HIRAETH

Selection of Poems and Writings

Robbie Sharma

Compiled by

Nath and Kiran Sharma

Acknowledgements
We would like to gratefully acknowledge the following for all their help and encouragement in producing this book:

Angela Sharma
Robin Heppenstall
J Wendy F Mills
The Revd Canon Gavin Kirk, Precentor of Lincoln

Published – 2007

ISBN 978-0-9554718-0-3

Publisher
Nath & Kiran Sharma
Coed Talwern
Dyffryn Ardudwy
Gwynedd LL44 2ER

Printers
Cambrian Printers
Llanbadarn Road
Aberystwyth
SY23 3TN

CONTENTS   Page

POEMS

On Faith

The Present Moment

To Anna

WRITINGS

Introduction

These poems have been gathered from Robbie's various diaries and notes; most of them have not been seen by anyone before. Many of them reflect his state of mental anguish - a crying of the soul for something out of reach. The essay on the Welsh word *Hiraeth* aptly identifies this longing for something that has gone or is just beyond us. Passionate about the Christian faith even in depression, he clings to hope, never doubting the power of love to transform suffering.

There are also poems on simple everyday events and human relationships, conveyed with tenderness and feeling, emphasising that such ordinary occurrences are an important aspect of life worth remembering.

The Writings are of a spiritual and philosophical tenor - there are four accounts of walks, which take the form of personal pilgrimage, with an air of adventure and spiritual aspiration. The essay "Christian Reunion" addresses the need to overcome inner and outer denominational division and fragmentation, and the play entitled "The Cathedral", no doubt, describes his condition, as he perceived it.

Robbie wanted his work to be made available to his friends and family, and to reach a wider audience; we are grateful for the poetry and writings he bequeathed to us.

Nath, Kiran & Angela Sharma

Foreword

Every person has a space between them and God. This applies to Christian and non-Christian alike. So much in life tries to make us either ignore or run away from this space. My poetry comes out of this space and is addressed to it. It is a *very* precious space indeed.

Poem

I want to write a poem
Yet my words seem
Only a faint echo
Of life and love.

I want to live
Yet my life seems
No more than a poem
Which will not rhyme.

I want to love
Yet all my love seems
Like longing for someone
Out of reach.

Robbie Sharma

On Faith

On Faith

Silence

Suddenly I heard silence.
And I knew God was there.
Suddenly all the noise of the world
Began to be rather less loud
Behind this awful silence of God.

So many people were hearing the noise of this world
And ignoring the silence which was there all the time.

Strange to Think

Strange to think
I'm a point of consciousness
So separate
From the others

Strange to think
My life means
So little
To so many

Strange to think
The way of getting through might be
Someone
I can't see

Strange to think
Of writing
And not
Telling

Strange to think...
Strange....

Music

It seems strange somehow
That wherever you look,
Out across the sea
Down an empty street
Out of the window of a train ...
Mostly, there's quiet.

The world goes on quietly
Massive acres of quiet space
Between towns.
And it can seem somewhat indifferent
To you, and you to it

And yet, if you can hear it,
There's music wherever you look.

Don't let the silence fool you
Listen ....

And hear the cadences of God
In the sea, in the Home,
In the fire.

It is possible to hear
Mighty chords
Or angels singing
Behind mundane surfaces.

What we call reality changes
And sings as it changes.

You

You,
Hanging,
Arms stretched out to all the world.

And now me,
Suffering at least with dignity.

The Precious Child

Through the pain and suffering of life.
And all that I have done to myself
There still lives in me
That poor, hurt child
Who is precious to God.

That child knows the beauty
And goodness of what is right.
And all the evil caused
By what hurt him
Has not touched that knowledge.

Now, at last , the child turns
And sees love shining
In the eyes of Jesus.
Now the child is smiling
Now his hurt is being washed away.

Your Peace

Bathing in the silence of Your peace
Small waves of love wash over me.

Stillness reigns, like a winter landscape.
Gentle grace murmurs
And I am made quietly free.

Like Snow

Like snow quietning a winter landscape
Your peace settles on me.

Beyond Emmaus

Lord, that day you appeared
To some of the disciples
On the dusty road to Emmaus
Was it a quiet day ?

Lord, I love to think of that meeting
On the dusty road.
Horizons of distance spreading around,
Emmaus still far off,
Jerusalem behind.

Lord, where were you going
Beyond Emmaus.
Why go further ?

It must have been strange
To feel again
Dust under your feet,
Feet having recently stood upon the vanquished body of Death.
Perhaps You wanted to tread further
To feel more the victory underfoot.
Perhaps you knew the business was not finished
And stretched far beyond Emmaus.
Perhaps that way lay the way back to heaven.

Lord, was it a relief
To walk again, the agony of death overcome ?
Lord, such a quiet meeting,
Such a dusty road,
To herald such a victory.

Lord, I somehow see you
As a quiet ghost
Looking far beyond Emmaus
To hearts that would welcome you
And to which You yearned to go.

Lord, did you see my heart
Beyond Emmaus ?

Jesus (after Blake)

Jesus ! Jesus ! burning bright
Through the watches of the night
Calling human minds and eyes,
'Taste and see and shine with light.'

In what distant hearts or minds
Has burnt the fire of thine eyes ?
To what heights dare he aspire
He whose heart has touched your fire ?

Ah! How human failings smart
And touch the sinews of your heart
And when your heart with sorrow fills
So ours with sins and worldly ills.

What the hammer? What the chain ?
Waits in hell these sins to pain ?
What the anvil ? What dread grasp
Dare its deadly terrors clasp.

As the world goes on in years,
And your fiery eyes are quenched with tears
Do you still smile your work to see ?
Did you who made the world want this ?

Jesus! Jesus! Burning bright
Through the watches of the night
Calling human minds and eyes
'Taste and see and shine with light.'

Shouting

When I see a man shouting
About religion
I ask myself how
He stays in touch with the quieter side
Of himself ...

The Question

To the question
What is truth ?
Jesus gave
The loudest silence in the whole of History.

Empty Words

What is this life
But a mist that appears
For a little while
And then vanishes ?

A man lives and dies
And the wind blows through the windows
Of his ruined house
Which remembers him
No more.

Yet while he lived
He spoke many words
Which came to nothing
Except echoes
In his sad ruined house.

Somehow the silence now
Underlines the vanity
Of all the empty words he spoke.

After Reading Psalm 118

Sadness speaks from my face
Yet few understand it.
For a moment I felt that in the end
The whole point of my being is to know God
To love Him, praise Him, and thank Him.

I am nothing, I cannot even trust myself
How many mistaken approaches to God

Have been made to the altar of my own self?

I believed, I wanted God.
Yet I did not trust Him
I prayed to Him
But I would not let Him answer
Because I was afraid.

Let those who fear the Lord say
With all their heart
His love endures for ever.

Let those in anguish cry out
And believe the Lord will set them free.

So Much of My Life

Lord, so much of my life
Has been spent in questioning
And trying to find answers
To great questions.
Now I know the beginning of wisdom is in knowing You.

I know, like Job, the futility of questioning
And I know the weariness of pursuing knowledge
Lord, I stand before you, one man,
And I stand in dust and ashes.

God's Love

God made this world
He made people the way they are
People that can love and hate
Kill, destroy, build
He knew the way it would be
The violence, the risk
The few takers of the offer
The few able to see

God's love is bigger than this world
Bigger than us, bigger than our failures
And our crimes.

Despair

Lord, my heart cries out in despair
When will you come to me
When will you deliver me ?

Lord, I cry and my tears flow
Please think of them, Lord
As the tears of the woman
Who washed your feet
And dried them with her hair

Lord, that is all I can do
In my despair …
Sit at your feet and weep
For the life I no longer want to live

In silence, Lord, hear my weeping
And take my broken life,
And my despair,
And make me new.

Hear My Prayer,O Lord

Hear my prayer, O Lord
And let my crying come to you.

For surely you hear the cries of the inner man
And you see the silent tears which no one else sees.

When it's hard to suffer
I try and remember your suffering

I think of you on the Cross
And the pain you suffered there

But then I think of the transfiguration
And how your face shone.

Lord Jesus, help me to remember that one day
All my suffering will be transfigured

Inexpressible joy will shine forth from my face,
Deep pain transformed into radiance.

Like a rainbow spanning a sad sky, sad no more
No longer sad, but beautiful.

O my Lord, I offer you my sufferings
Please do not forget to transfigure them,
One day.

I Will Sing

I will sing, O Lord
O Lord, I will sing
With my faint and broken voice
I will sing.

My voice trembles like a reed
Because it can hardly bear
Its song

Yet as the gentle breeze
Moves the reed
So your song comes to me
And claims my voice.

I will sing, O Lord
O Lord, I will sing
With my faint and broken voice
I will sing.

How surprised I am, how honoured
That Your song finds me
Poor singer that I am

My eyes fall to the ground
Staring at the dirt
Looking away in shame

How can I open my mouth
When I am so afraid ?

How can I sing your song
When it finds in me
So strange and barren a land ?

Yet I will sing, O Lord
O Lord, I will sing
With my faint and broken voice
I will sing.

Poor, lost child that I am
I wander from place to place
Trying to find eyes that will recognise and find
The child in me.

Wherever I go I find instead
Ears waiting to hear
A strong and vibrant voice, a strident song.

Yet all I can give is what I have …
Only a gentle song
Only a broken voice.

And You command me,
'Lift up your eyes, take heart
I will give you a song to sing.'
I will sing, O Lord
O Lord I will sing.
With my faint and broken voice
I will sing.

Angels Dancing

I have seen angels dancing in the sky
I have seen the angels dancing

Beyond the empty faces, cardboard smiles
Beyond the harassed souls

I have seen angels dancing in the sky
I have seen the angels dancing

Beyond the voiceless singing of songs
Beyond a silent crying

I have seen angels dancing in the sky
I have seen the angels dancing

Beyond a furrowed face absorbing pain
Beyond sightless eyes

I have seen angels dancing in the sky
I have seen the angels dancing

Beyond, beyond the crawling now
Beyond rain tomorrow

I have seen the angels dancing
Dancing in the sky.

Standing Silently in Church

Standing silently in church
I see many different kinds of people
By seeing them, their faces, their expressions, their walks
I get to know them and love them.

I like to know they are there
They are my Friends
I like to think I know them better than they know me.

There is a silence, a space between us
My shyness will not bridge
But somehow I'd like to preserve that space
Although it sets us apart, it allows God to come between us.

Lord

I don't know you, Lord
For all my attempts,
For all my desire to know you
I do not.
I do not understand you, Lord
I do not understand the suffering
And the pain
Why do you let it happen ?
Especially to those who are trying to love you ?
I do not understand your absence
From my life.
I am confused, and near to despair
I have reached the end
Of months and months of trying
Of trying to replace despair with hope.
I do not understand theology
It seems so irrelevant beside
The common problems of humanity.

Yet, although I feel hurt and bruised
And fed up with You and your demands
And your pain-filled world,
If it comes to a choice between
Misery and gladness, between despair and hope
I will chose Hope.
There is a burning flame within me
Which remains alight, aglow
And which refuses to die.
Why is it so hard for it, this flame ?
Why is it so weak ?
Why am I so weak ?

I Made You

I made you
I delight in you
I delight in what you are
The way you are
I delight in your babyhood,
Your childhood,
Your adolescence
Your coming of age
I always love you
I don't stop when you do
I can't, I don't know how to stop
I can't help myself
I just have to keep loving you
Whatever you do or don't do
Whatever you do, I already knew
I knew your failures and your successes
Don't think, in your pride,
That you can do anything for me,
I may do things through you, that is all
But first of all I made you to be you
You are enough as you are
Just live, just be, just breathe.

Chapel

As I sat in the chapel
I felt a sense of peace and light and space
And in the silence my candle burned
And the sunlight fell through the window

As I left, I noticed how beautiful the sky was
With the bright sun and cotton-wool clouds
Lord, I know that somehow we try too hard
And in our obsessions we destroy the thing we crave.

You come in gentleness, in little things,
In peace, silence, stillness, love and joy.
You are what we notice out of the corner of our eye
The suggestion of a fragrance, almost a by-product of effort.

And I feel I would rather be a doorkeeper …
Rather visit you in your temple each day
Than get obsessed with my own efforts to reach you
To give thanks for the small things, and to love simply.

O God

O God
Though you may send years of pain
May I never lose the heart
Which at a single soft touch from You
Will flower in love, and shed the memory of pain
Because You remembered to touch.

O God
One day in Your presence
Will surely transfigure a thousand days of pain
And then the question with which I ached
Will be answered.

A Flower

After much suffering and much striving
I kept my soul tranquil and quiet
To hear the whispers of God.

And like a gentle breath they came,
Like the breeze touching a flower
They touched my soul.

Where for so long I had striven so hard
And crashed with heavy footsteps of seeking
There, gentle and lovely He came into view

Without seeking I found Him at last
The wayward vision came aright
And where was darkness, now gentle Light

So, like a flower you must be

Hold yourself upwards to the Light
But do not strive too hard to grow, for grow you will

And surely you will glide towards Him,
He who tends and gardens you
And weeds out all that hinders.

And remember who made the flower
Will also harvest it, it was not you.
And please, as you go, be fragrant.

Judgement Day

O God
On judgement day
I will not cringe and cower
Or be bent by tragic thought,
Of the way my life might have been

I have done many things wrong
And failed to do much that could have been good.

But then it will all have passed away.
I will remain
Appearing out of a mist of memories
Into the reality of the present
The person You made
Yet with some good qualities You gave me.

I will not speak
I will simply look at You
And the expressions in our eyes
May exchange a smile in silence
To smooth over the receding anguish
Of a life lived and over.

I will be hoping
You will remember the little things I did
To bring a smile to peoples' faces
The little things which were at times
All I lived for

And the smiles I managed to give
When in pain
Which became a sort of vocation.
And the love I felt for people
And the world.
O God remember these.

To The Unseen Friend

My dear friend
I am too weak to go on
You must go on without me
Fight to the end
And do not forget the love which burned
In my heart for you
Remember me sometimes
Remember I cried and laughed like anyone
That my heart was big
Like the mercy of God
And that in the face of hell
I could still sing, trusting in our Father

Well, now you must go on
Leave me and do not look back
To where I lie.
Pray often for my soul.

The Present Moment

The Present Moment

Today

Today
Today's reality is what I find
Is all that is available to me

Today
Comes like a ghost,
An echoing shadow

Today
Is today's feelings, thoughts
Emotions

Today
Escapes like a thought
Dissolves like a dream

Today
Is failing, growing, becoming
Knowing,

Today
Having gone by
Adds itself to the growing pile of my past.

Early February

Today the sky holds a promise
Of other places, other times
That is not now.

A time to be quiet, a place to rest
My soul yearns for that place, that time
But now there is only the noise of now.

High Clouds

High clouds in a blue sky
Advancing into the distance
Seem to speak
Of far horizons of the soul

And the spaces before them.

Clouds Over The Wash

Cloud arches across a space of sky
In a way I can't describe
Except to say
The sky is big, the sea flat
And the sky a space full of hope.

The clouds' endless rearrangement
Seem like ideas for today
And they herald their own gigantic presence

A great black tower's menace dissolves in rain
 'There is only now',
Only an eternally changing pattern of Hope
Happening now.

Ebb

Life, from day to day,
Ebbs away.
It fades, like a beautiful dream,
We cannot hold it –
We can only add
The perfume of our presence
To our slipping bequest.

Outside My Window

A raindrop on the rose branch
Outside my window
Is like God's tear
Shed for this tired world.

The gentle breeze in the trees
Across the lawn
Is like God's tenderness
Stirring in my heart.

The view of distant hills
Across the down
Is like a glimpse
Of eternity beyond passing clouds.

The robin alighting on the post,
The butterfly settling on the flower,
Are like the fragrance of your love
Coming to my heart in silence.

Approaching Autumn

The wind is blowing in the trees
The leaves are falling

Life is moving on
Change is in the air.

The wind is blowing in the trees
The leaves are falling.

Meeting Pain with Hope

Meeting Pain with Hope

I Would Rather Run

I would rather run for days
Against the wind and the rain
And the mad sky
Run until I fall, than face
The torment of this dark, encroaching future.

Like the dark lapping lake
It washes the silence of my present.
Like the shouting sea
It rages.

I must gird myself about
With qualities of adaptability and resource:
Still the great cumulative depth
Thuds dully with the changed,
Softly saturates new flashes of old moments.

So I must run
Until this keen alertness wears;
I may glimpse from the frayed edges
But not frightfully stare
At its violent accelerations.

Like the dark lapping lake
It washes the silence of my present
Like the shouting sea
It rages.

To Be Quiet

The thing to do is to be quiet.
To stem the volubility
Of solitary words
Repeated arguments, undoubtedly right
But uttered, like flimsy windbreaks,
Against the great onrushing eddies of experience.

Now producing a momentary sense of rightness
In understanding being wronged
And now opening themselves up
In allowed glimpses, then in full desolate truth,
To show the futility of speculation in the
Aftermath of hurtful contingency.

The thing to do is to be quiet
To immerse the partially self-shattered mind
In mundane task after mundane task.
Let it mend itself
Let the overarching vision
Bring into focus the disparate pain
And dissolve in the moving now

The past shouts sometimes, and
Sometimes cries,
Mourning out its dismembered memories
In disquiet parody of their lost reality.

Pain

Sometimes
You suffer so much pain
That there is nothing to say.

You can only smile
And gain dignity.

The Blind Woman

The blind woman waits on the platform
She is still,
And her white stick straight.
A man helps her to the train.
I am blind like her, but I have no white stick.

Condemned

Condemned,
Ever to speak, no-one hearing.
Condemned to walk alone
Separate and apart,
Communication lines broken,
But the need for love remaining.

My own prisoner.

Yet all prisons fade,
Love melts bars.

Another Winter Comes

Another winter comes
And shakes more leaves
From the gnarling tree of my life.

Twig-black against the paling sky,
So are the scars on my soul
That another aching year has left.

Yet I feel a certain beauty
In the scar and in the ache.
And in One to whom I can only
Offer them.

Meeting Pain With Hope

It is here, this time
It is now.
It is with me
It is forever with me.

And I go on
Meeting pain with Hope.

Passing Shadow of Pain

I will laugh
I will smile
Through the passing shadow of pain.

Oh Lord, may I never lose
The feeling that peace is possible.

Showing You Cared

Today
On my way home
A wave of loneliness
Swept over me.
My lips trembled
And I had tears in my eyes.
I also felt gratitude
And thought of You
On the cross
In pain, in agony, and lonely
Like me.
Showing you cared
For just such a time as this
And a person such as me.

Sometimes

Sometimes
I can see myself
A great lumbering shadow
Coming up out of the mist
Going through life
Looming up into the street
And fading forward to a dark future
Not really knowing
How I got here
Or what to do, now I am
But always going forward
Lumbering, lumbering on

I can be relied upon
To keep going
A moving shadow
Against the world.

Don't Lose That

Life is hard
Yes, life is hard.

But there is still softness
There is still softness.

Don't lose that.
Don't lose that.

People will hurt you
Yes, people will hurt you.

But there is still gentleness
There is still gentleness

Don't lose that.
Don't lose that.

Clouds will build up
Yes, And rain will fall

But there is still a rainbow
There is still a rainbow

Don't lose that.
Don't lose that.

The world is full of pain
Yes, the world is so full of pain

But there is still a smile
There is still a smile

Don't lose that.

Don't lose that.

We will age and die
Yes, We will die

But there is still love
There is still love

Don't lose that.
Don't lose that.

Failure

Have you known failure?

Yes, I suppose you have.

Ah, but have you also seen
Rain-clouds roll aside to reveal
A sun no less brilliant
And with the same smiling shine.

New Hopes

Like breezes billowing the skirts of a tree
So, this year, new hopes rise in me.

They rise like sunshine spreading over a meadow
They dissolve old burdens of pain.

Springing up towards the smile of love
My hopes come, rebuking memories of disappointment.

When I Was In Pain

When I was in pain
A daffodil's quiet still yellow
Comforted me.

When I was in pain

The sound of rain wetting the window
Calmed me.

When I was in pain
I remembered an old illness
And my mother reading to me.

When I was in pain
Echoes of old griefs
Returned as friends.

When I was in pain
I became still
And listened.

When I was in pain
I felt love squeezing
Out of me.

Oh God

Oh God
Please restore the dignity of my soul.

The hail of occurrence
And the thousand natural shocks
Have done their best to bruise and hurt

And yet I stand
A hurt but humble soul
Before you.

Take pity on me, O Lord.
Restore my smile
And let the deep waves of sorrow pass.

All I am is yours
And I offer to you
The beautiful echoes of sadness
In my soul

And as a strangely wondering child
Discovering peace after a storm of tears
I thank you for still holding me.

He Knew He Was Dying

He knew he was dying
But knew it was better to die in the body
Than in the head, or the spirit.
His condition, which he could explain
Intuitively and intellectually,
Yet somehow not really get across to anyone
Would not take too much scrutiny.

Let go of possessions
Which cling like barnacles
Take to the upper air of the spirit
Of values, love and life, joy and peace
Establish bridgeheads against an unknown future
Journey and seek
Keep hope alive with courage
Live each day as if it were your first and last
Love God and others too more than yourself.

London Life

London Life

London

I am torn by you
Discarded, Abused by your violence
Tossed about in your tumult of change;
People after money
People impelled by profit, lust, power, greed,
Selfish energy.
Broken, violently broken
I am, you are
Dying, people, loveless eyes
Tramps, homeless young, the discarded
People asking for 'ten pence'
People closed off from each other
By their greed, their rushing.

Fallen out of the general desire
I am lost, left out, alone.
Dirty, untidy streets
Reflect people's lives.
Ceaseless traffic, ceaseless noise
Always digging up streets
Always movement, never rest.
No home, no community
No love
In this city, humanity is dying
In pockets it raises up its hopeful, cheerful face
Defying the deadening weight
Of enemies seeking to crush it.

In this city the kind word
Between strangers has been lost
And greets instead
Friendless stares, empty eyes.

City Violence

It's not so much
The physical blows that hurt
The reports of old ladies
Attacked, beaten by youths

But the way senses are raped
By the protrusion of violent images.

So many shops with bright lights
Superficially welcoming
But staffed by ear-ringed youths,
Not quite there to serve you.

Fast cars driven by inconsiderate people
Impatient with obstructive buses.

There's too much transport in this city
And not enough arriving,
Not enough getting there, and being still

Always travelling, tiredness mounts
But, unacknowledged, it finds expression
In the irritated word.

The Onward March of Progress
(In the style of Shakespeare)
Adapt, adapt, adapt
And stem the choking tide
Of hurtful new experience.

But, when you have done so
Take care lest your conscience
Steal a glance
Back over the gaping spaces
You have otherwise filled out.

There lies the remains of slow compromise
It is the deserted meeting-place of old and new
Where continuity was betrayed.

Something is Being Lost

Something is happening in Britain,
People are going so fast
They are forgetting something about themselves
It will be dangerous to leave behind.
Something is being Lost
It may be hard to retrieve.

Vanity

'Vanity, vanity, all is vanity,' saith the preacher
Words, Words, words, words, words.
People talking
Using words,
But I hear not the words
I hear the voice behind the words
The voice of vanity.
It is the person talking, the whole person
A person wanting to be heard
With opinions, ideas, thoughts, visions
Each person a persona
Whole, complete.
Word-spitting, saying they know
And the vanity is violence to my ears
A cutting, screeching violence
Because these people are saying 'I know, I know, I know so much'
But what use is their knowledge ?
They are violently, vainly speaking
And their speaking is not energised by love;
Their words fall dead on unloved ears.

Power

So many people
In one way or another
Want power.
It's a mainspring
That drives so many.
For many people it defines the course

Of so much of their lives
The people they'll talk to, and why
And what they'll get out of it.

If what lies behind so many words
Were uncovered
Would we have bothered to listen ?

Shout

I am going to shout in this poem.
With a six cylinder voice
Not angry. Oh no. Not violent …

That's not my public face.
No, for me the measured written shout
But shout it is nevertheless.

Life

I feel as if Life left me behind
Some time ago.
I find myself in groups of people
Who seemed to have moved on
To be further forward.

But, strangely I'm still here
Although behind, I'm still amongst
The wreckage of a life still floating
And still hoping to reform.

Oddness

Everybody's odd:
We get stuck in
The safety of sameness
The Lie of similarity
That denies the flowering of variety,
The setting free to be me
In my wonderful oddness.

You and I

We're in this together
You and I,
This thing called LIFE.
Whatever I do or achieve
I do on the same stage as you.
We were both born, will both die.
We've a lot in common, you and I.
In between , little differences of make and circumstance
And big differences of WILL
Will mean we'll steer different courses.

Life Goes On

Life goes on
And the effects of decisions deepen.
And the shadings and tone of things,
Like how a person says 'Good morning'
Or a subtle grey sky
Matter more.

Office Space

When you work in an office
You begin to notice spaces in your day
Reservoirs of needed peace
Compensating for the turmoil of work,
Calm islands in a rough storm
You keep arriving at only to cast off again
And which have become important to maintain
And come back to.
Like waiting for a train
Or walking in the park at lunchtime.
Surrounded by work, office core time,
They become precious, needed.

Office Girl

I used to work in a room
Where there was a girl who used to come in sighing,
Looking hassled and heavy

I didn't know then
The depth behind these sighs
Or the difficulties and decisions
Underneath her pleasant smile.

Since then I've seen her
In corridors and lifts.
She always smiles and says hello.

I feel I know her
And the cry which rises from her.

A Smile

Within a crowded day at work
I went to get a cup of tea
And at the hot water point
I met a girl who smiled at me.

Her smile was the best thing that happened that day.
How beautiful just a smile can be.
She smiled as if to say,
'What fun just to meet, how lovely'
Just like that, for a moment
As if she was happy to see me.

I'm grateful to her
Because her glance brightened the whole day.

Office Knight

Yesterday,
On my way to work
A girl asked me if I knew

Where the 'Inner London Probation Service' was.
She was almost crying
And may have been late.

I said, 'I am not sure that I do,'
And she carried on, a forlorn figure,
Along Great Peter Street.

Remembering, running back, and saying
'I do know where it is'
Was a tiny rescue
By an inadequate Knight.
Seeing her undisguised tears, a blessing.

How beautiful is admitted weakness
And often demands more courage
Than keeping it down;

Compassion welled within me,
She seemed like a sad daughter.
I wanted to do more for her than I could,
Like carry her there -
Or buy her a coffee
Until her tears had gone.

I left her to turn back, hoping
I'd got it right
Compassion subsiding as I entered my office,
I went in again to the world of false strength.

Young Poet

Now I have become a not so young man
And, education gone, I am uneasily engaged
In the world of work,
To which education seems now a largely irrelevant hinterland,
I find it is easier to pretend to be a poet.
Experiences others have, perhaps unconsciously, sacrificed to
Tight schedules and deadlines,
Seem to lodge with me and remain
And seek expression.

On the Way Home Today

On the way home today
I passed some beautiful people.
They were just ordinary men and women
But they were beautiful.

I missed the stop on the tube
And finished up in Finchley West

I went home and prayed,
A friend came, the evening passed.

And now, before bed, I write these lines
Not knowing quite what happened so special.

Going Back

Going back to
Work on the sixteenth floor of an office
At the end of an impersonal corridor
In the city
Looking out across a hotch-potch of buildings
I can see the roof of Buckingham Palace below me.

I felt jarred back
To a hard reality I half-welcomed
At least it gave stability
At least it was a job.
But the other office-workers
Seemed different.
They seemed like rabbits
Burrowing in piles of paper.

And, having been disengaged from this game,
Coming back to it was strange
I saw reality stripped of its reasons
I saw the horror of the building
And people not communicating
And their need to disguise
In pretend interest in work.

I saw people huddled in trains
And people stepping out of rooms
Into corridors, ignoring each other
But I didn't see a justified why
Any more.

16th Floor Window

There is a blue sky over London,
And white clouds with flat grey bottoms
Are floating silently over the city.
From my 16th floor window
I see calm silence gently resting on chaos.

Docklands

Sliding out of Bank Station
On Tuesday
On the almost noiseless DLR
I glide up to a privileged view of Limehouse squalor
… Into the eerieness of Docklands.

Beneath a cloudy grey sky
There is a scene like a 1950's film, modernised:
Quiet housing estates, new railway,
Shiny new office blocks, the docks,
All Saints Church.

It's a brave new world out here
But there's a feeling of familiarity,
Traditional sounding East End voices.

Despite the developers' rubble
Which seems to mirror something in me,
Perhaps the scattered landscape of my past,
Still littered with the rubble of broken events.
The offices are like isolated islands shorn up by money.
And the council estates part of the debris,
To which I add my preconceived impressions.

Emma's Departure

Emma left today.
She had the front flat.
She was a girl I spoke to only twice
But now she's gone
I miss her voice.
She had a young girl's voice
Which sounded friendly
Coming through my door
When she came in up the stairs.
She had young friends
Including a boy friend who stayed the night.

Although I don't know for sure
I think she came from Kent
And was a student;

Her things have gone from the bathroom we shared.
I used to imagine what it would be like
To have a girlfriend's things in my bathroom.

As I came back from the park
Where russet leaves carpeted the grass under the trees
And a clear Autumn wind waved the branches
And a girl sat on the bench reading a newspaper,
She and a friend who called her 'Em'
Were loading a small van in the road.
From inside I heard them moving things down the stairs.

I wish Emma well wherever she is going
Even though to me she was only
A voice on the stairs.

Cherry Tree Wood

It is one of those still November days
When a peaceful silence seems to rest on things.

Children playing in the park,
White gulls loitering on the grass,

Flat puddles reflecting sky.

I am reminded of the depth behind things,
That there is a loneliness in life.
We inhabit vague spaces,
Sometimes seem only to scratch the surface

Of who we are,
Or were meant to be.

But sometimes there are meetings,
Connections,
When silences, pains of years bear fruit,
When the air seems thick with promise,
And perhaps a soft sky spreads hope.

Motorway Poetry

That Friday afternoon, leaving London
In a borrowed car,
Hertfordshire surrounded the motorway,
Hurtling cars, arrow-like, to the north.
The weekend rush had already started
Under a pale February sun.

Great green swathes of land
Were a relief after urban tightness.
It seemed strange that no people were there –
After the aimless wanderers you see in London streets.
Why not come out here, to space ?

To right and left,
Hills smoothed to majestic woods,
Clothing their shoulders,
Latticing the sky.

I listened to some music on earphones,
Dire Straits, Prokofiev, and a choir.
In places I sang along
Watching the mirror to check
No-one could see me too closely.

The music shrouded the incessant sound of tyres on tarmac.

At Birmingham, I caught the rush hour
And crawled, ant-like, in a herd of vehicles
For an hour.
All about, a calm industrial wreckage
And a factory called 'Fort Dunlop'
Formed a view.

Later, I became slowly aware
Of a heavy grey, weighting the sky.
As I drove forward
The green of fields, and the remains of blue in the sky
Gave colour, and the rain-clouds seemed to herald
The North.

On that journey, my car sealed me,
A speeding observer,
Catching glimpses of so much quiet land
And houses, outside,
How much poetry did I catch, I wonder
And how much was I too fast ever to have noticed?

View to the Fens

View to the Fens

At Denver Sluice

The wind rustles leaves
Of Riverside trees

The water is calm
And the swans silent.

The gentle breeze in the trees
Seems to signal the freedom of the sky

The silence of the fens
Seems to sit on the land
Like a mantle
Sometimes brooding, sometimes beautiful

Gaunt houses, gates on banks
Stark against the sky

Birds calling across the flat miles
Lamenting the loss of the sea.

They seem to welcome me
Deep their loneliness
And mine.

Lights of houses bursting over fields
In the evening haze.

This is an understated place
Where you're not quite sure if you've caught
Its message
Or what it is.

You feel it is saying something to you
In its silence
Or its quiet tones

But you feel it may take years

To find out what.

This coming back seems to say
Memories don't have to be painful.

Whatever happened then
This place is still part of my past.

A setting free from the past
A washing of old wounds.

A Prayer

The weeping willows sigh
By the lonely river
In the midday silence

On the opposite bank
In the high trees
Birds sing and call.

This place with its quiet water
And its air of loneliness
Its stillness
Calls to my soul.
The lonely places of my soul.

The silence of this place is deep
Like the space left by
Huge displaced water
Something has been lifted from here
Allowing it to wait (in silence)

This place is a prayer
I have walked into,
A whispered prayer.

A River in the Fens

Outside,
I can sense,
The wind's desolate moan
Passing through dark-shrouded trees

The day's peace
Has become an intense loneliness,
A space uninhabited by love.

Oh love
Come and warm again
This lonely place
Where birds call and swim.

Light

A gunmetal sky waits,
Light is stretched out
Like a clear thought.

Across Norfolk

Yesterday the wind was blowing great white clouds
Across Norfolk.
Their shadows raced across the fields
And floods of sunshine lit up the earth
The beauty of this glorious vision shone
And the landscape seemed clean.
In hedgerows and on hills
There was a profusion of blossom,
Pink of cherry trees
And wonderful shades of white
Adorning spider-thin lattices of branches.

And in the sky sometimes behind the clouds
There was a rare and gorgeous gold
A brilliant streaming forth to earth.

The Iron Dome, Earith

The breeze is blowing softly
Through the summer-faded green grass
To produce the echo of a sigh upon attentive ears
For those who no longer inhabit the dome.

The sigh shivers around the metallic frame
Which stands atop the occupied and deserted tumulus
In whose time-carved culverts
Cows transform the grass and daisies into peacetime milk.

Through the trees and brambles
Lies the ageing land, traversed by quiet rippling waters near at hand,
Twice reclaimed from powerful enemy,
Natural and Unnatural.

Time's dustiness has killed the mechanism
Of this revolving tool of hurt
And only hide-and-seek eyes
Occasionally glance, now, through the gaping gunport.

Man's whim, relayed in higher spheres,
Has changed the function of this former watchtower,
Now watching only over children's play on the Washes
And the play of sunlight on the straight-directed water.

View to the Fens

At the end of a wet Sunday afternoon
I went for a short walk
And passed the Hall and Rectory.
They seemed, against the wet grey sky,
Caught in the silent void of Sunday afternoon.

Just off the roundabout and main road
The Hall and Rectory stand like islands of the past
Still clinging to their roots.

Away out beyond the town
Across miles of fen land
Lies my old village.
At the boundary of an old county,
On the edge of the school catchment area,
At the edge of vast flat fens.

Here I became a connoisseur
Of silence, fen land and loneliness
How rain can wash the sky
How flat water reflects back light

And how the soul aches
Which contemplates the water-displaced land.

After many years I found you could see
The cathedral tower, ten miles away
Across the fens from the flood bank
At the village edge

And the shape of the land
Became clear to me
And the displaced water
Like the bird whose flight
Reveals the Ship of Love.

Song of Life

Song of Life

The Great Space

Trying to encapsulate a great space
In the soul
In words
Is like trying to bring into view
A hidden depth
Trying to make public
A private world
The hinterland of my present
With all its decisions, and loves
Which have made me what I am.

Or have they ?

Does life make us what we are
Are we moulded ?
Does ' what happens to happen' mould us to a shape ?
Or does a person's character somehow create his life ?

Or do we come to life
Already a person
Only waiting for events to give our stamp to
Decisions we make ?

The great space remains,
Silently echoing with life.

Space and Silence

A space surrounds each of our lives
We talk, love, work, play
Go on journeys, and come to rest.

There are periods of noise.

But always the space, and silence, return
And we come back to ourselves,

Finding again the wonderful aloneness of our lives,
That we grow with our own bloom
With an individual fragrance, unlost
Amongst the places and the people
We belong to.

As we grow older
This space hungers more to be filled
With something not ourselves
And hungers to be given, lovingly given.

A Love

Stretching across the scars of life
There is a poetry, a love
Which soothes and heals
And makes us whole.
It is like a sweet breeze
Delicately reappearing
In times and places
We perhaps least expected.
It gently holds the failures taken
In rushing forward perhaps too fast
And reminds us that our lives are not our own.
Love does not depend on us, on what we do
It is there always, silently remaining
Waiting for us to come back
From our preoccupations and obsessions.

Old Songs

The old songs are best
Their melodies seem an echo
Of something already heard
They come back like old friends
Lighting up new pain.

When life is hard
And goes on being so
You have to just wait

For the old song to come back
And until it does
You have to remember
The old song's echo.

Fresh Songs

Finding a voice
Finding a way to flow
Fresh songs to sing
Is a way of finding life.

It Sings

There is a magic in life
That is as old as the hills
And the sea.
It keeps vapouring back.

We get bogged down
With money, power, sex
And we can no longer hear life
Singing.
Oh it sings! It sings!

Everyone Has Their Poems

Everyone has their poems
Little things they scribble down
From time to time
On buses or the loo
But how many of us
Are poems ?
People who are always happening
Always flowing
Living in rhythm
Singing their lives
Being instruments of love
Being the big thing
In the simple way?

Oh! How many of us dare ?
How many ?

A Poet Must Sing

A poet must sing
A poet must always sing
Wherever he finds himself

Whether it be in flames and darkness
Or the wreckage of a life
Or in glorious light
And the bloom of life
A poet must sing.

Saxophone

What tune can I play
To the silence which surrounds me
How can I accompany myself ?

I seem to hear the lonely echo
Of a saxophone.

What sound comes back
From around me
What sound comes back ?

I seem to hear the lonely echo
Of a saxophone

Can you hear the sound of my life
Coming over the fields of sorrow
Already turning, already tinged with joy ?

I seem to hear the lonely echo
Of a saxophone.

Have I Sung in Vain

Tonight I cry for you my friend
I cry for you
Who are alone like me.

Tonight I am alone,
In retreat from the noise of the city,
The rush of the day

Like me you are alone now
Gone in from the noise
And again alone with yourself.

Will my song find you, my friend
In your silent room
Will my voice carry ?

Have I sung in vain ?

Song

When I feel I can do
Nothing
When my heart is overflowing with
Sadness
When my eyes can see only
Darkness
When the rainbow does not
Arch
Across my failures

Then I want more than ever to
Find
The song that sings of beauty and
Love.

Sighing for the Past

Sighing for the Past

Back to Lincoln

Coming back to Lincoln with my mother
After fifteen years
It seems to have waited patiently for us
Familiar buildings still stand
And cherry blossom and rain
Adorn the old streets.
Old faces appear, some I've never spoken to
Yet I feel I know them.
There is always, for me, an air of welcoming expectancy,
Of praise and joy.
It seems to be there, too, out in the villages
Harmston, Navenby, Dunholme,
And old Skelly !
Even in the hedgerows and the woods.
And in the golden rape fields
Smiling at the sky.
There is a breath of home here.
I see the house where I was born,
My mother points to the window.

History breathes here !
Medieval monuments mediate
Echoes of a Roman past
Of Lindum Colonia.
Old ladies who seem to have been here forever
Inhabit old houses around the cathedral.
Yes, I would drink a cup of kindness
For the sake of old times in Lincoln.

Coming out of the cathedral
I see white clouds slowly drifting
Across wide blue Lincolnshire skies
Coming in from the North Sea
Across the East Midlands
Here to this place where History breathes!
Where the old stones hold echoes of a past
Bathed in antiquity

The clouds drifting high above the cathedral
Are magnificent!

Pilgrim Way (All Saints Church, Harmston to Lincoln Minster)

The birds are singing on a day
The sun is streaming down,
As I walk the onward pilgrim way
Through countryside and town.

However heavy is the load
Which weighs a traveller down,
The breeze comes blowing light and free
With grace and peaceful sound.

Passing of My Childhood

I lament the passing of my childhood,
How innocence has flown.
I remember spaces I played in
Bereft now of my excitement
And those who shared it with me.
Those spaces now seem to contain
A quiet sweetness,
There before I came and there, still.

A Copse Where Children May Have Played.

What affection may have warmed this copse
In eyes glancing and going back
At the quick leaf-wrapped steps
Caught on a sparkle of pristine memory.

How lonely it is now, to me,
Stark against the dull sky
Above a folded dell in the grassland
And nobody in sight in the still winter.

Return to Ely

Coming back here
I sensed space.

The familiar streets and houses
The cathedral, the school -
They welcomed me,
Old things unchanged.

I wondered if I could live here now,
Start afresh, with a new heart
With optimism and hope –
I wondered.

I seem more and more
To seek and need a home.
Does this mean I need one more
Or that I'm less at home in myself?
I wonder (about this).

The river is silent -
Groups of ducks and swans
Glide freely in flat silence
Cows graze on the flood banks.

In the evening
Lights come on in isolated cottages
The silence, although soothing, is lonely
Although it's there for a purpose –
Distant from us

My memories of here are tired
I've thought on this place so much
I wouldn't like to admit how much
Turned pain over and over
Until I've tired it out.
Thinking of what might have been
Yet how useless that is.

The silence sits here
There's time here to spend a lifetime
Turning over one failure

There's a brooding feeling
Across the flat landscape-
The sky is too open; too vast.

A Journey's End at Ely

Once, by day, I laughed and shouted
Up on the hill
Under the Cathedral shadow

But now, by night, I stand on the station platform
At the bottom of the hill
And see the glow
Of the lonely signalman's cigarette.

Waste Places

The waste places of life
Resurface
In warm memories,
Empty and with no significance:

Love, a slow and gentle breathing,
Warming and melting,
Redeems the wasted and insignificant.

Years Afterwards

Have you ever felt, years afterwards,
The space behind a man's tears
Or the touch of gentle words ?
They have not been lost.
They have left the sweetness of a memory.

Nothing we ever say is lost.
No tears are cried in vain.

Words, tears, come back
Again.

Wilderness

In every life there are wilderness years
Things get bigger, rules recede, old boundaries dissolve,
And we are led out into a vast space of opportunity
Life really is what we make it.
Through the wilderness we need both light and faith.

Sighing for the Past

Sometimes I sigh for the past
And wonder what might have been.
It is a sweet sadness
For life gone by
For tender feelings
Which lay along things,
Things now past or lost.
As the tenderness of those feelings has flown.

Regret is useless.
All will one day pass away.
Suffering will be transformed
And that tenderness will come back.

Recollections of Light.

Now the rooms are dark,
The curtains drawn.
Outside the thick night cloaks
And the warmth from the fire
Glows on our enchanted faces

The rooms are light
And silent
The dust falls shadowless
Through the gliding rays
And a ghost is there.

Sometimes

Sometimes
When I look at my past
I seem to be
A ghost,
Haunting certain roads, certain rooms.
That memory contains not me
But someone I was
And who now exists
Only in a memory
Only my memory
And that of the haunted.

Go Back

Who will go back ?
Who will return

To the dusty covers
Of my life ?
The days
Which still have about them
An openness
An accessibility to the age of memory
Who can go back there
To my past
Except I
Only I.

The Park

Sitting in the park
I saw light and gentle April leaves
And pink and white blossoms
And a rich and fertile green.

There was a tranquil space here
And life was going by.

I thought my cares seemed too deep
For the surface of this afternoon.
Why have I become so lost
In my deep self?

Tears came to my eyes when I saw
The boy kicking the football with such energy.

Old Man

We met in the street
The old man and I
He grasped a stick
And an old man's bag
And Time, insistently pounding,
Was shaking his face to remind him.

We met in the lane
The old man and I
He stumbled along
His thoughts shambling too
And Time, his eyes blinking slow
Had streaked his face with use.

We met in the meadow
The old man and I
He picked a daisy,
Stepped in a fairy-ring
And Time, making him forget,
His flowering youth he remembers yet

The lines of care which surround
The dimly glowing eye
Fold into smiling flesh
When his memories sigh.

While Walking

While walking
On a sunlit morning
I called in at a wayside house
Facing across the valley
Towards a hill before the horizon.

The old man sat
Motionless, facing the wall
Looking away from the humming summer scene
Outside,
His thoughts were passing slowly,
Slow as the summer was changing,
As his slow breathing.

I filled my water bottle,
Stirring the warm silence
With my clatter,
Thanked him,
And left him alone.

A Trip to Oxford

On the train
Familiar fields passed by
The train was quiet
After the noise of shabby London Tubes
And I was moving to a quieter place.

In dark November Oxford
The station had been rebuilt
A taxi took me to St.Giles
Where I had an appointment to keep.

Walking back later
I saw a familiar face
I passed without saying Hello
But felt comforted by his still being there.

Glancing down Broad Street
Yellowing walls seemed to glow
In the friendly incandescence of shop lights
I felt warmed by a swathe
Of remembered times wrapping round me
'This was air I once breathed,
Streets I once walked'

Now, for me,
A train back to London
And an insignificant chair
In an office.

In Hiraeth (Wales)

In Hiraeth (Wales)

Dyffryn Beach at Easter

Looking along the beach
Sea and sky and sand merge
In a brilliant meeting of light
Reflected from the wet beach.

The sea wash-washes the shore
Gently, gently,
Again and again
A slow, persevering attempt.

And a seagull lands on the wet beach
Looking this way, then that
Surveying glory calmly.

Easter Birds

Today I saw some birds
Flying together against an ash grey sky
Their dip and rise seemed so full of joy
Why not fly ? And why not together ?

Swallow Falls

The waterfall washes over the rocks
Like a million gallons of milk !
It is an unceasing roar
Which neither recedes nor fades.
Like a foreground echo, displaced,
It continually surprises my senses.

In Hiraeth Amongst the Hills

If I could walk here
                    In Hiraeth
Amongst the hills

If I could sing here
                    In Hiraeth
To an open sky

If I could love here
                    In Hiraeth
To the answering heart

If I could die here
                    In Hiraeth
Free as the wind.

Spain, India & France

Spain, India & France

SPAIN

Sea

Sea chop, sea mop
Up the tourists' debris
Onto the pebbles, sand and shingle.

Sea fine, sea define
The contours of the headlands
And the bays.

Sea sigh, sea shy
Sometimes in raising up
Your voice of power.

Sea low, sea show
Us the beach you have left
For our Footprints.

Sea high, sea fly
In endless crashing perforce
Dying over the rocks

Sea bobbing, sea sobbing
Through the days
For the tears of clouds –

Sea Vast...

Spanish Plain

The evening silence surrounds
The spires soaring to the sky
From the Spanish plain.

They reach into the beautiful blue stillness
Bastions of Hope set against the sky

And the peace of God lovingly surrounding them
In the calmness of this evening.

So my soul would soar in hope
To you, Lord.
Leaving behind the enemies of its stillness

I reach, like the Spanish spires,
And like an immovable rock I set my face
Towards you.

I run from the plain towards the sky
My soul on fire with the thought
Of your love.

Bach, By Chance, in Figueras

By chance we drove to Figueras
In the morning instead of in the afternoon
And wandered a way through the milling streets
Towards the memory of a son of the town
Born to fame in a surreal spasm.

And hard by the arranged museum,
Its founder dead, and the colour of the pictures
A little faded now, which each day
Swallows avid staring eyes and gapes
Into its bizarre capitalist throat
Tinged with egg-white and snail blood,
Faces the sacred edifice of Figueras.

Borne to me on the modern Street gazes,
Was a strain perhaps I recognised,
And Mother thought, and the tunes
From the endless repetitions and practice-sessions
Came back, and she said it was Bach:
Toccata and Fugue in D Minor.

We entered, and as the wind slammed the door
On its hinge behind us, the sound amplified,
And the differently stained glass

Set in the high tradition-glowing stove
Threw back the organ tremor into medieval cadence.
And, for the duration, there was no questioning,
No longer any doubt; how could this power,
Which has the power to enhance the common prayer
(carrying wind-wards on its flying assembly, and avoiding stumbles and
repetition, and thoughts of shops and dinner)
Be not divine; and certainly the felicity of its movement
Shows an inspiration begotten of a faith
Such as the inductive faith in day and night.
I would say I have sinned
I would say Christianity has power,
And is not dead in the heart;
I would like to whisper, amidst tears and wailing and penance,
To the reverence and sublime pathos of the Hanging Figure.

And after this, the bathos of the Museum.

INDIA

Maharashtrian Evening from a Railway Carriage

The evening silence intertwines
With the peacefulness of dust-settled roads
Overhung by motionless leaves whose shade fades below.

And the sound of a calmly- pedalled
Black - bicycle wheel does not penetrate the vast silence
As its transitory particularity is absorbed into the eternal dusk.

Distance on the plain is filled
With air of shadowy density
Which human eyes may not disturb

But still above, the sky retains a violent spectrum
Of fantastical cloud-shapes, ragged blood streaks yellowing,
Arranged in a half-forgotten childhood dreamscape.

Colva Beach (Goa)

Fine sand, scuttled by the brittle legs of sprinting crabs,
    so small before the arc of
                the Vast Arabian Sea,

and smoothed by the incessant water - lap,
    rocking to and fro in the cup of its
        oceanic bed, at the dictate of a silent planet,

in a narrow strip, tapering a portion of
    the subcontinent into the
        silent submarine world.

The final presentation of those
      parching rays is here, and a
        more aristocratic dust –

before the subdued heat drowns itself, and
    the shadows extend beneath the palms

and the undersides of distant clouds retain the fading image of the day

conveyed across the miles of barren loneliness
    accompanied by cool wind rushing low,
        the support of reclusive wings

which beat and glide that distance
        to chance a salt and silent glimpse
                of the airless world beneath.

their being is ours
        as our individuality recedes
            with the waves.

FRANCE

Driving on French Roads

Driving on French roads
Columns of trees on either side
Herald our progress.

Cloud massifs drift silently
Above poppy dashed fields

The diesel drone of big lorries
Going west.

Tree shaded roads
Gently waving leaves
Softly swaying trees
Filtering sun from sky

In deserted squares
Flags draped hotel de ville.

Channel Crossing

Starting on deck in the dark
I am drowned by a sky deep with stars.

The boat is moving evenly through a calm sea
And the lights on the French Coast recede.
Approaching England,
A lone lighthouse flashes silently
Like a mute ambulance
No need for sirens at sea –
The dangers here are hidden and silent.

And, answering, these flashes in my soul
A repeated warning.

I am going back to difficulty.
The difficulty of the here and now, of reality.

Friendship, Family and Love

Friendship, Family and Love

Grandma's House

I am sitting in a chair
In my grandma's house
Reading a book.

I was so sensitive then
I looked out of her window
And into the garden

It was as if you were there with me
As if your love now touches a place
Long ago where my grandma cared for me.

To Alka (a cousin)

Sad and happy morning maid
Remember that meaning's made in the masquerade
Of life.
You may choose your purpose or your end,
And thus infuse an overtone of self-control
Into the subconscious.

But better still preserve the challenging uncertainty
Of spontaneous action tuned
To the mainstream.

And finding it better so, to glide along,
Without the deadweight distractions of policies and
High Ideals,

You will proceed with silent gravitational rotations
Through the mysterious days and nights
Of perception.

Towards a goal unseen and unattracting,
Eventually receiving you without disappointment
Or regret.

You

You laugh
And somehow, when you're there
We want to laugh with you.

You bring sunshine and love with you
Flowering in you
So beautifully

You're so sure and in control
I don't envy you
But I'd like to share in you.

You are someone
I'd like to follow
Hoping

The shining light of you
Might release me
From my dark self.

You're so beautiful
Has anyone told you ?
Do you know ?

I'd like to tell you
Just
To make you happy.

I'd like to be alone with you
And just
Talk.

All embarrassment lost
In knowing
You.

Dear Sister

Dear sister
I know your pain
And I weep for you.

Your sad head hangs down
And you get so tired
You seem so helpless
Sometimes ready to die.

I knew the depth of your sorrow
When you said 'I want to die'.

I weep for the lovely girl
Beneath the deep pain
A girl with long hair
And shining eyes, ever faithful.

I often wish I could be
A kinder brother
And I think how tragic
Are the unspoken words of love
And the spoken impatience and irritation
Instead.
And how they have hurt you.

I pray that you will know
Yourself redeemed
From all your pain
For all eternity.

Dad

Shaking your hand this afternoon
Made me want to cry.
You were always there
To sort out my problems
When I was a child.
But part of me didn't grow up
And I have managed to make a big mess

Of life.
But I still hope
In the sadness of what I have done
And not become
That you can sense a thank you
Filled with brimming tears.

Daddy, you gave me life
That was the greatest gift
That could be given.
I was too proud, too proud.
Yet I still hope my life can be redeemed
If someone else, not me, could be
The redeemer.

I See

I see a great and empty space
A dark cavern
Aching with need

I see a great darkness
A dark shadow
Crying out for light

I see a guardian at the gate
Knocking, knocking
Waiting for an answer

I see a lover
Whose heart is overflowing
With a most beautiful love

And then I see the lover
Bend and kiss
Space and darkness, filling them with light.

Waters of Love

Let hope rise in your heart like a springing well
Let the water of new life flow
Drink deep, and let your soul be filled
With the waters of love.

'You Have Your Own Fragrance'

' You have your own fragrance'
You said one evening,
And I felt it resting on me
Seeming to bathe me
Clothe me,
How lovely to feel one may have
A fragrance to others
A sweetness rising out of
The way one is.

I Love You

When you said
'I love you'
You touched something
Inside me.
I wanted you to touch it
Again
And I asked you to say again
'I love you'.

How I needed to hear
Those three words
How we all do.
To know we are loved
Is worth more than worlds.

So Much in Life

'I love you'
Ah, those words.
They carry so much
Besides their plain meaning.

So much in life
Rests on things unsaid
Things words carry besides themselves
Somehow, love's presence
Is not a matter of words
So much as the air
Or something else
Being right.

Love blows where it will
It may come to you or me
Today
It may be carried in my words
I pray love may visit you
Quietly today.

Romance and Love

Romance and Love

She of the Sweet Voice

Today
She of the sweet voice
Rang me up.
'Hi darling !' she said –
My heart melted.

'Is she as lovely as she sounds?' I thought.
I could listen to her voice for hours -
Brightening up dull old minerals.
When she laughed, I caught her joyful chuckle
And I wanted to make her laugh again.
'She's a lovely lady', I thought.
And I asked God to bless her.

She Rang Again

She rang again yesterday.
She said she thought I was an angel
Because
After everything she said,
I just said 'Right'.

Could I say something else,
Like 'OK Yah' ?

I said I wasn't a yuppie.
She said she thought
I was well spoken, though.
Impulsively, directly, I said
'You've got a very nice voice yourself'.

'I'm melting here'.

She asked if she could ring again.
I said 'Yes'.

Her voice was balm to me.
I couldn't think of right or wrong
I needed her lovely soothing tones.
I just wanted to listen silently, like a baby.

I said I was tired from lack of sleep last night
She said she wouldn't ask why.
Then she got embarrassed, and the conversation ended quickly.

Checkout Girl

Yesterday
In Sainsbury's
You looked at me.

My vision was almost too full
Of piles of food and people
But
I caught your glance
Despite.

I thought a girl like you
Deserves flowers
And soft music.

Instead of flowers, your fingers
Moved goods,
And all your music only
The bleep of tills.

To … Love from Home

My love is blowing in the breeze
Scent from flowers, blossom from trees
Far away across the seas
To the place where my love … is.

I can see her now with her smiling eyes
She's quiet, and I am by her side
She is so gentle, feminine, understanding me
Love surrounds us and I say, simply, …

From a lane near the house where I was born
Where horse chestnut blossoms dance in the sunshine morn,
And peace, beauty abide, blue sky and breeze
I send my simple longing love to you, ...

I Can Feel You Here

I can feel you here,
You have gone
Yet I feel your presence,
Like sweet perfume from a flower
You have left behind you
Your loveliness in the air.

My home is peaceful --
In the dusk I sit on my bed
Where you sat too.
I still feel your love here
In this room, and that one too,
I wait here quietly in the summer dusk
Thinking of you, letting your love touch me.
I feel your sweetness and how gentle you are.

For ...

The wind blows in the grass,
The summer air blows free,
The hills in the distance call to me,
As through long hours alone I pass.

She is so very far away,
Like horizon in the distant haze,
Yet far is where I long to gaze,
Remembering where I fell in love one day.
I long to be close again with her,
As a simple word or look touches my heart.
I long never from her to part
And never from Love's long gaze to stir.

My Love

High trees of early summer
Sway and dance in a breeze.

Hanging over a lovely green field
They drop fragrant petals.

My memory haunts that spot
And remembers the breeze
And the trees
And the soft fragrance of the petals.

Will you come, my love
And walk with my memory there.
Will you stand there, innocent and wondering
As a child,
And catch the fragrance
In your breeze blown hair.

And will you simply feel
The presence of my memory
Loving you.

To Anna

Our Eyes

I look into your eyes
And we hold each other's gaze,
Sometimes looking away shyly

In moments we recognise something in each other
Our whole faces smile

Your eyes are free and clear and blue
Like sun-drenched sea,
Yet tinged with grey,
Like a summer sky etched with the beauty of rainclouds

My eyes are brown and dark
Like the earth,
Needing you to water me
With the loveliness of your grey blue gaze

When I am away from you
I can feel the smile and the warmth and the love of your eyes
Shining back through mine like an afterglow

You transmit your love to me
Through your eyes and into mine,
Warming me inside,
Making me glow

Just one reason why
It is wonderful to be with you

You make my brown eyes blue.

Hello

When you say "Hello"
It is like a ray of sunshine,
A gentle thrill of joy,
A singing hum.

Your voice is fresh
As if you are pleased to be addressed,
And hope your Hello
Will bring back a smile.

Your "Hello" is so simple.
I am here, you are saying,
And if I can,
I will make you happy
With a single word.

I Folded You In My Arms

I folded you in my arms
Like a delicate flower.

I held you gently
Afraid of my strength.

I released you,
Like a song carried on the breeze.

I Have Grown Large With Love

I have grown large with love.
Nothing else matters but this.
All my conceits are blown.
I am in touch with the invisible force
Which drives everything,
The strange and mysterious power
Which it is life's purpose
To be at one with.

And when we are displaced
Or removed from it, like strangers,
Our purpose is only to seek it again,
Our instinct always for love.

Across The Hills

I imagine myself
Walking across the hills with you
Across fields and beneath the trees.
Hand in hand
Our eyes meeting
Our lips touching.
We are smiling at each other
Happy to be with one another
So very happy to have found each other.

We lead each other to love's horizon
Gently touching each other with our presence
Each to the other.
We are sometimes gentle and sensitive
Which makes us catch our breath.

Will you love me for ever
In the dew of the dawn
When the sunshine makes things bright and sparkle?
So that I am never alone,
Never without you.

Stay With Me

Stay with me
Till we meet again

Stay with me in your mind
Think of me and keep me close

Stay with me in your heart
Feel love for me from afar

We are apart from each other
But distance falls around us

Creating the space to see clearly
The shape of our presence.

In Lincoln Cathedral

We walked in the Cathedral
Where I had been a choirboy
All those years ago

I was so sensitive.
I wish I could love you
With a childlike love now.

I lit a candle and placed it in the sand
And you sat down near it
And I followed you.

I held your hand
And looked into your eyes.
You said it was our candle.

Two children placed candles in the sand near us
And then they knelt down to pray.
I knew God was hearing them.

In those moments
I saw simply and gently
That you loved me.

I saw it in your eyes,
Not a great revelation
But a simple and gentle thing.

I felt in touch with myself,
My real and childlike self.
And I felt the same simple love for you.

The prayers included ones for those we love the best
And love the most.
I prayed for you.

WRITINGS

Hiraeth

The Welsh word "hiraeth" has been defined as a longing for something that has gone or is permanently out of reach. A symbol for the word has been suggested, by a different writer, in the cry of the curlew. One can imagine hearing the cry of this bird across a heather landscape at dusk, a cry containing within itself the suggestion of an echo, and being reminded of an area of one's heart that was either forgotten or covered.

Yearning and longing come from the desire of the heart. As the Prayer Book confession tells us, it is possible to follow too much the devices and desires of our own hearts, and Jeremiah warns us that the human heart is both ambivalent and treacherous. It is therefore possible for desires to be base or corrupted. Yet it is possible for our deep yearnings to rise up from our souls like the cry of the curlew, sad in awareness of their base origins, yet seeking to rise through articulation and through direction to something beyond themselves.

St Paul, in Romans 7, powerfully describes the Christian anguish, almost schizophrenia, of human nature divided between attachment to sin and the freeing of the soul from the body of death through the spirit of Christ. In Platonic philosophy too, ethical absolutes are identified, to which imperfect human desires may aspire and rise.

We yearn from the sadness and the bearing of our individual loneliness for the warmth of love. Our souls yearn for a stable and permanent home from which they cannot be swayed by desire. A lasting place of rest and of peace from earthly striving. There is a dignity in articulating the cry of our souls. We somehow know, deep within, that earthly greeds and possessions will not ultimately satisfy. It is as if we remember having once been in the womb of God and yearn ever to return to that place of love and warmth, as to a mother.

Nothing articulates the cry of our souls better than music offered to God in our great cathedrals. In its sadness and joy, in its quietness and volume, in its quality and in its crying. "Hear my prayer, O Lord, and let my crying come unto thee" sings Purcell's anthem. Such music evangelizes and energises the soul, and leaves an echo of the presence of God. And it points beyond itself to the music which underlies all our actions.

Lincoln Library
21 September 1996

On The Quality of Silence

I would like to consider three types, or qualities, of silence. I will begin with the sort of silence experienced within the enclosed interior of a church or cathedral. This is a silence given shape or form by the surround of an ecclesiastical architecture and stained or clear glass windows. It is a silence rich with spiritual significance and historical depth. It is a silence which may have deepened, like a reservoir, over many centuries. It is a silence with a hinterland and an echo. One of our great cathedrals, perhaps, on a quiet afternoon, or a deserted parish church.

A different quality of silence is that which can lie or hang over a landscape. Here, it can be punctuated, perhaps, by the intermittent cries of birds. This is a thick natural silence which almost seems to emanate from the land itself. Let us think of remote parts of the Fens or of the Pennine hills, or of the Lincolnshire Wolds. Yet this does not seem to be a silence of desertion but of a strong presence. Walking on the Hambledon Hills one summer, I experienced a silence so thick and pregnant with presence, it could almost be felt and handled like a living thing.

Let us now think of a small room. I have in mind a room where I once stayed in France. There was little furniture and the walls were wood-panelled. Long shuttered windows opened out on to a courtyard, enclosed by a wall. Below the room was a small stairway, leading to what had been stables. Sitting alone on a chair, I felt this room hiss, buzz and hum with silence.

Here we come to the paradox – the sound of silence. What is the relationship between silence and noise? A still, attentive listening to silence seems to produce an awareness of a seemingly psychic hum, which accentuates and clarifies the silence, and prompts us to consider whether there is such a thing as absolute silence. John Cage's silent musical piece indicates the meaninglessness of music without the punctuation of silence. And the insidious bleeping of modern technology and the proliferation of background music and other noise, shows a lack of concern for the social value of silence.

Silence is related to Action. There is something slow about silence. There needs to be a slowing down to experience it fully. If silence allows us to become aware of ourselves, then surely our obsession with speed and noise indicates our fear both of silence and of genuine self-awareness. We might distinguish the "confused action" so prevalent in our society – a succession of tangled, half-completed tasks – from "controlled action"– a series of slow, silent, methodical actions completed in due order, one at a time.

But above all, Silence is related to Love. Consider the dignified beauty of a man or woman (or for that matter an animal) in silent motion. Or of two people sitting in a room, wrapped in a silence pregnant with love.

Cambridge
13 November 1996

St Francis

"N-no problem", said Francis with a slight stammer as the latest person de-posited their post. This was his usual way of indicating, at the conclusion of an exchange, that the deposited postal item or items were safe in his hands and would be dealt with and despatched in the appropriate manner. There was, however, just a hint that items which Francis verbally stamped "N-no problem" did nevertheless represent part of his hidden weight of responsibil-ity. If, on the other hand, he ended an encounter with the more cheerful, "Okeydoke" you knew there was something lightweight about the matter, either physically or administratively. Francis used two other stock phrases with great regularity. These were: "'Ang on a minute", when the build up of imminent tasks had to be slowed down, and "I'll do me best", when the ur-gent or last minute request had to be met with willingness, but not promises to do the impossible.

Francis usually wore blue trousers and shirt, with brown safety boots. Often in the morning he had a dishevelled appearance, rather like a child who has dressed hurriedly without a mother's help, his shirt collar half turned up and his dark, greying hair a little ruffled. He shuffled a little, and stammered, and was disabled down one side of his body so that his left hand tended to turn back on itself. Everyone called him Francis, though his real name was Frank, as if in recognition that the halo of peace that seemed to surround him could only indicate a saint behind the mundane reality of a franker of mail.

Sometimes, when he came to rest in a quiet period in the usually busy Post Room, Francis' face seemed like that of a cheerful and willing, but slightly saddened donkey awaiting its next burden. He had a good sense of humour, and one day told a true story about a nervous Italian burglar who had taken tranquillisers and subsequently fell asleep on the job and woke up in the local police station. He told the same story, with slight variations, to about six different people at intervals during the day, and each time accompanied it with a deep doubled-up laugh to go with the hearers' smile, as if to say, "What you find amusing, to me is hilarious." In his spare time Francis played bowls, and went rambling and cycling.

The Post Room, like Francis himself, seemed to have an air of peace about it, which settled back into place once the dust of each hectic phase subsided. There was a long sliding metal doorway at the end of the room which opened out on to a view of house and trees and a sky, which often seemed peaceful too. As people came and went with their mail, during the day, they greeted Francis as if he was a permanent and loveable fixture, a receptacle not only for post and packages, but also for smiles and scurried gratitude.

Who would want the social respectability of a job in high finance or the law when they could have the privilege of helping a saint sort mail? Stamping the first class, entering the recorded delivery on the computer, changing the sacks of mail when full up, punctuated with an "'Ang on a minute", or "Okeydoke". What could one do, but one's best for such a man? The meek shall inherit the earth. Meanwhile, they do the real work, and do it with humanity. And just as you're about to walk away thinking the exchange over, true to his own slow rhythm, half a moment behind the beat, Francis will gently stamp his mark: "N-no problem".

Cambridge
9 October 1996

117

The Cathedral – a short play

Scene 1: Outside the Cathedral

Narrator: It was a cold winter's night, and the fog swirled about the old cathedral on the hill. The streets round about were deserted except for one or two people; the cold seemed to have driven people indoors. It was a scene that might have been taken from the end of the nineteenth century, and the fog made the street lights glow mysteriously, as if they might have been gas-lights.

A young man came slowly through the great arched gate in front of the cathedral, stopped and stood still before the great edifice. He looked up at the doorways, arches and windows, and he seemed impervious to the cold. Then, as if from nowhere, a woman appeared. Even in the dark, it was obvious that she was of fair complexion and great beauty, and her face glowed with warmth despite the cold. Then I heard the woman speak.

Divine Philosophy: What are you doing here?

Man: I was looking for you.

DP: Well, by chance I happened to be passing this way, and I found you staring up at the sky. Why were you looking for me?

Man: I was thirsty.

DP: Do you think I could quench your thirst?

Man (distantly): You do not know how I have thirsted for you, how much I have missed you.

DP: Are you sure it is me you are thirsty for? Not, perhaps, some alcohol to drown your sorrows, or have you already been drinking some of that?

Man: Oh no! I have tried that method - it doesn't work. It only adds a headache and wasted time to an unchanged problem. My real thirst is for you, and always will be, in spite of my baser nature.

DP: Well then, perhaps we had better go inside and sit in the warm. Then we can talk more privately. Not that there is anyone about here - it is too cold.

Narrator: I watched, as the two of them approached the door of the old cathedral and go inside. As they disappeared the fog seemed to deepen as if denying there had ever been two warm-blooded creatures in that vicinity.

Scene 2: The Lady Chapel, in the Cathedral

Narrator: I followed them into the Cathedral, and saw that they had gone into a small chapel, the Lady Chapel, at the back of the Cathedral. I could hear them talking:

DP: Why do you thirst for me?

Man: Because I have committed a crime, and I am in a dilemma. There are no easy answers to it, and to help me I thirst both for wisdom and for the presence of someone who is good.

DP: Tell me your crime and your dilemma.

Man: You must understand that I cannot be specific. I have committed a serious sin against God, what the Catholics call "a mortal sin". This will certainly have serious spiritual and psychological consequences both for me and probably for others. The seriousness of the crime is hidden from others, yet is clear to me. Even allowing for false guilt, I am certain that I have not exaggerated it. The dilemma is therefore how to act for the best.

DP: As you were speaking, it occurred to me that I could suggest to you some principles, which might help in resolving this dilemma. Perhaps it will help if I explain these principles to you before you say any more about your crime or your dilemma.

Man: Yes. I think it will help.

DP: First, Humanity: whilst admitting and taking personal responsibility for our own sins and shortcomings, it is good to remind ourselves that we exist in solidarity with the rest of mankind. Second, Honesty: it is wise to aim to tell the truth about what we have done and not to evade it, deny it or dress it up as that which it is not. We should seek clarity and not confusion.

Third, Appropriateness: we are wise to consider how to speak or write about ourselves, who to and at what time - our words should be appropriate both to ourselves and our situation.

Fourth, Communication: it is right to communicate our error to an appropriate person and to God. Communication opens the way to resolution and proper perspective.

Fifth and last, Transcendence: we should seek in our actions, words and prayer to transcend the prison in which our errors would confine us. We should seek out how best we may do this in our particular situation.

Narrator: When she had finished speaking, which she had done clearly and firmly, there was a silence whilst the man seemed to consider and weigh up all that she had said.

Man: Thank you for explaining these principles to me. I have heard it said that right action is based on true insight and not simply on knowledge. I wonder if you could explain some philosophical principles to me which might help me to distinguish right action through true insight?

DP: Yes. I will. Consider your duty by cultivating an objective detachment from your situation. Endeavour to observe the possibility of the existence of absolute standards of value whilst allowing for the practical application of those standards to your particular situation. Have faith in spiritual values and uphold right reason as its measure. But in matters of moral judgement, apply the logic of imperatives rather than deductive or inductive logic. Listen to your conscience and consider the practical wisdom of tradition and of the community.

Narrator: Again, when she had finished speaking, there was silence for a space before the man spoke.

Man: Thank you. Now I want you to leave me here a little while, to think and pray.

Narrator: I saw her get up gracefully and leave him sitting there alone.

Scene 3: The Chapel

Narrator: After she had gone, I saw the man sit in silence for a long time lost in thought. Eventually he knelt down and prayed, sometimes whispering. I saw that he had tears in his eyes and occasionally he gave an exclamation. Then I heard the woman's gentle step as she re-entered the chapel and sat quietly at the back, waiting until he saw her.

Man: I am glad you have come back.

DP: How are you feeling now?

Man: I feel a little better for seeing you back with me again. A number of thoughts came to me whilst you were away. Would you mind if I shared them with you?

DP: Please come and sit beside me and tell me what they were.

Man (going and sitting beside her): It occurred to me that, just as Socrates' wisdom consisted in his knowing that he was not wise, so my own goodness consists in my knowing that I am not good. I have been granted an innate capacity for insight into this, whereas most people apparently do not appreciate their lack of goodness. Similarly, the very fact that I have met you here enables me to see, by contrast with you, the absence of goodness in me.

Narrator: After he had said this, there was a short silence. They seemed to grow closer as they allowed the silence to go on between them, even though they were sitting close together. Then the man carried on speaking.

Man: I also thought of this cathedral. As a child I sang in this place and acquired a spiritual perception, which slowly grew into a vision. It was a vision of truth which I loved, and because of this I became a philosopher according to Plato's definition. But at that time I knew nothing of Plato. I only knew that, side by side with my childish nature, there was a philosophic vision capable of great and profound insight into spiritual and human reality. It was as if my mind and heart were lifted up to God in a kind of contemplation, which occurred simply because I was here and a part of the life of this place. I really believe even now that I was able, in a way, as a child, to understand profound spiritual mysteries.

Narrator: Again, he stopped speaking and there was a silence. I noticed that now there seemed to be tears in Divine Philosophy's eyes, and she took his hand and put it in her own. She seemed very beautiful, and in her shadow he, too, seemed to become handsome.

Man: I also thought of this: I believe that I was given a gift through this place and my association with it. It was a gift of love, a sort of spark of divinity which made me capable of being close to God. I somehow understood how God could love people as a father loves his children, apparently distant, yet with a deep and abiding love. And I was capable, through this gift, of being moved to tears through my heart, simply by hearing the sound of a person's voice, or a strain of music, or the sight of a landscape. I understood somehow that these were all dependent on God and all symbolic of Him. God was in them, and they in God - and I had the gift of immediate apprehension of the connection and its significance. The connection and its significance is Love. Love is everything. An individual gift, but of social and ecclesiastical significance. My crime is that I allowed damage to this priceless gift. I cannot articulate either the crime or the dilemma in words, yet I know what it is. And I know that I would rather die than allow any more harm to come to this gift, or bring shame or dishonour to the name of God by speaking words which cannot convey truth.

Short pause

Narrator: After he had finished speaking, there was silence.

Short silence.

Lion Yard, Cambridge
14 November 1996

A Letter of Tentative Reflection on Two English Cathedrals for a Foreign Christian

During 1992 and 1993, I had the good fortune to attend services at Westminster Cathedral and at Westminster Abbey regularly. I work in Westminster in a Government Department and so was able to use my lunch breaks to attend services. Occasionally, I also attended Evensong and the Sunday morning Eucharist in the Abbey. I am a lover of cathedrals. I love the sense of grandeur and the power of the organ and choral music. I love, too, the sense of space and the majestic stonework, and the feeling that one is in a many-roomed house, a sort of mansion which is a symbol both of heaven and of the richness of the human soul.

Going to the two different cathedrals in Westminster gave me the opportunity to contrast and compare Anglicanism and Roman Catholicism, as represented in these two places. It is difficult to be precise about the differences – they are differences of texture, ethos, style, atmosphere. There is a more mystical (is that the right word ?) feel about the Cathedral, the Abbey is more down to earth. The Cathedral is of course a more modern building, and is unfinished. From the outside it looks Byzantine (as indeed it is), and inside one has this magnificent view, straight down the nave, towards the wonderful overhanging Cross with its beautiful depiction of Christ in an attitude of sorrow and love. This is a tremendously powerful image. It seems as if Jesus is shining out of the darkness of the dome behind – it is dark because of the unfinished ceiling. Perhaps it should be left as it is, as a symbol of the darkness of the human soul with Jesus in front, at the 'gateway'.

The Cathedral is quieter than the Abbey, and people seem more reverent. There are also more candles, which surely cannot help but give a greater impression of warmth and vitality. The liturgy of the Cathedral revolves around the Mass, and I have enjoyed the lunchtime Masses. Sometimes they have got a bit dull, but usually I have enjoyed them. It is an impressive sight watching queues of believers going up to receive the Body and Blood of Our Lord in silence – only the sound of feet and the sight of faces. It is wonderful to reflect on what is happening in people's hearts at this time. I have also found it powerful to hear the Gospel proclaimed, but proclaimed quietly and in an orderly way. The quality of the homilies has usually been excellent, and it is interesting to gauge a priest's character by his diction, his gait and his examples. Westminster Cathedral is a haven in the midst of the ugly facade of Victoria Street. To find this quality of prayer, worship and silence in this location is a miracle.

Westminster Abbey is, as I have said, more down to earth. It is of course much older, having been founded by Edward the Confessor as a Benedictine monastery in 1065 – a year before the Norman Conquest. From the outside the masonry seems to shine, now that it has been cleaned, to a sort of milky white. Inside, one wonders at first whether one is in the house of God or a national museum. The first thing one sees is the Winston Churchill plaque surrounded by wreaths, and one immediately notices how full of tourists the Abbey is. One has a distinct sense that the church and the world meet in Westminster Abbey, and I can't help feeling that too much of the world has been allowed in. If Jesus were to return and go into the Abbey cloisters, surely he would be angry at the marketplace which has been set up there.

Perhaps as an Anglican I feel as if I know the ethos of the Abbey better than that of the Cathedral, and so its weaknesses annoy me more. If that is so, I am still very enthusiastic about its strengths. The choir is excellent and Evensong is a wonderfully reflective, meditative service with passionate singing. The Choir of the Abbey is more intimate than the nave of the Cathedral and has a homely feel about it. The clergy appear to be warm and dedicated and indeed the spirituality here is something intimate, something indistinct from the place, almost oozing out of the old stones. The service sheets are clear and well printed and the healing services on the first Wednesday of each month are very good, as are the Sunday morning Eucharists. The weekday lunchtime services are sometimes frustrating, because of the noisy tourists.

The Abbey is clearly a national church, which claims also to serve the Commonwealth. It betrays the Anglican identity, which combines Christianity with Englishness in a way in which the Jews might be said to have combined Judaism with Israel. There is undoubtedly an "English genius" in the Church of England, but one feels that a regeneration and renewal of the specifically Christian is needed – Christ must come first, English identity second.

A Canterbury Journey

Between Epiphany and 10th of January, I went on a journey on foot, through the snow, from London to Canterbury. For some time I had the idea of doing such a pilgrimage sometime between Christmas and the Week of Prayer for Christian Unity. My aim was to follow the Pilgrim's Way, which medieval pilgrims would have taken, and I started from Southwark, having spent some time the previous day praying in Westminster's Cathedral and Abbey and the Methodist Central Hall chapel. I took various aids to prayer with me, including especially the verses from Ephesians 4, which seem to make it so clear that in the true spiritual sense there can be no denominational division:-

"As a prisoner for the Lord, then, I urge you to live a life worthy of the calling you have received. Be completely humble and gentle; be patient, bearing with one another in love. Make every effort to keep the unity of the Spirit through the bond of peace. There is one Body and one Spirit – just as you were called to one hope when you were called – one Lord, one faith, one baptism; one God and Father of all, who is over all and through all and in all."

I said these verses as a prayer in the churches I visited on the way and also as a sort of chant whilst walking. Believing that there should be an ascetic element to my pilgrimage, I slept outside at night using only a sleeping bag and a plastic survival bag.

The snow seemed to have an exhilarating and purging effect. The Pilgrim's Way itself became like a friend, faithfully leading me across an apparently impassable landscape. I caught the medieval 'feel' of the Way in places, as I found my way along paths which had been covered with snowdrifts and across roads where cars had been abandoned. Yet although alone I did not feel lonely, and there was a magical feeling in the white silence.

I had been struck by the sense and depth of peace in the cathedrals and chapels of Westminster and Southwark. It was the same in Rochester, where I arrived in a Dickensian dusk, and at Aylesford Priory when I arrived in freshly falling snow. The interior peace of these places was complemented by the peace of the snow-covered land, as if to remind me that Creation preceded Revelation and in the primary sense of Creation, there is no ground that is not consecrated. A well-known walker has said that Ecstasy is an unfashionable commodity, yet as I slept on a snowy hill above the Medway outside Rochester one night, I was buoyed up from the cold by some such transport.

But on the third night of the journey, the cold caught up with me. Despite careful precautions, I felt that I had overdone it and I had to light a small fire to keep warm. I was prompted to feelings of sorrow and repentance, and the next morning was forced to abandon the Pilgrim's Way, because the newly fallen snow was too deep to permit anything other than very slow and arduous progress. After a meal in a roadside restaurant (deserted except for a wonderfully friendly waiter), I walked the rest of the way to Canterbury along minor roads and arrived just in time for the Cathedral Evensong, having walked for six hours almost without stopping. One of the prayers was, "Lord, where Your Church is divided, unite it in Your Love."

The final lesson came the following day as I sat in silence with a Christian friend. I was acutely aware that this was the true end of the journey – friendship and a loving heart – and acutely aware of the connection between our mutual silence and that which I had experienced in the peaceful churches and the silent landscape. God was with us now, and He had been with me there alone. Yet I had only come to realise, or perhaps remember, this silent loving Presence through the failure of my individual efforts to stick to the Pilgrim's Way, and through the return to relationship.

My friend reminded me of Chaucer's Prioress, "Amor vincit omnia". I thought of T S Eliot – after all our journeyings we shall return to the place where we started and know it for the first time. Is it possible for the divided Christian denominations to rediscover the love which can only come from a united heart ?

A Lay Christian - 1997

Christian Reunion

"May they be brought to complete unity to let the world know that you sent me and have loved them even as you have loved me". Jesus (John 17 : 23)

John 17 makes two things absolutely clear: Christian unity is God's will, and it is fundamentally related to love. Let me add a third consideration in the light of 2000 years of evangelism: we should speak now of Christian Reunion rather than Christian Unity, a coming back together rather than a coming together for the first time.

Do Christians really want Reunion? I sometimes feel that Christians, in their natural desire for security and refuge, allow their emotional sensibilities to become institutionalised and spiritualised within a particular church tradition to a degree which makes the idea of Reunion threatening. Perhaps people confuse the comfort of the Holy Spirit with being comfortable in a settled mode of church life. Yet given that Reunion must be God's will for a divided church, surely every Christian must strive to overcome personal preference for the common good?

Perhaps it is worthwhile reflecting on the distinction between God's will and our will, and between the emotional and spiritual. Becoming a Christian is not primarily a matter of an emotional falling in love, but rather of a spiritual reorientation of the will. God gives us free will to respond to His grace, recognising that we remain distinct from Him. If His will is Reunion, surely we must direct and rule our wills to conform with this, putting our emotions in second place. Yet it is we who have caused the division, so it is we who must do the work to bring about Reunion - both practical work and the work of prayer.

Why should Reunion matter? I want to consider five points to try and show why it matters very much indeed:-

1) A soul may be lost because of disunity.

> A Catholic writer has said, "The Catholic Church ... has not yet reached clear understanding of the extent of the loss which a church suffers by the fact of its separation from Rome". In trying to find its way around the denominational maze in search of authority and truth a soul may become confused, disillusioned and may abandon its Christian journey. Alternatively, caught on the barbed wire

of institutional division, a soul may, faced with the necessity of decision, leap the wrong way and seek to accommodate itself to a truth whose shape and feel do not fit.

2) Denominational division results in a fragmentation of Truth.

What was clearly intended (from Scripture) to be one whole Truth becomes divided. This results in doctrinal distortion and theological bias.

3) Disunity grieves the Holy Spirit.

The Holy Spirit is the Spirit of Truth and always tends to bind together in unity of love. The Holy Spirit continues to yearn for reunion where division has occurred because God cannot disown Himself. This is perhaps particularly so in the case of the Catholic and Anglican, Catholic and Orthodox, and Anglican and Methodist communions.

4) Disunity often results from an individualist tendency which undermines the sacrificial character of the Church.

St Augustine said that all sectarianism is self-justification, and it is possible to see the same principle in the self-assertive individualism of modern times. Yet much more fundamentally Christian is self-sacrifice for the sake of unity and the common good.

5) Disunity is the single biggest obstacle to true and effective evangelism.

What right can a Christian have to preach a gospel of love and unity when this is not in evidence in his own society? Who will be convinced?

St Irenaeus said that the glory of God is Man fully alive - not partially alive or alive to a partial truth.

I would like to make a proposal for Christian Reunion. First, the deliberate taking up of the idea and concept of Reunion - of coming back together again in love. Perhaps a subsidiary concept might be the French "rapprochement". Re-approaching each other. Yes, cautiously and carefully, but also alive to the potentiality of what love can do to transform an apparently intractable situation. Secondly, I would propose gathering together at the local and at the national level for the purpose of sharing a meal - not primarily for worship or for prayer, but for the simple physical act of sharing a meal and exchanging the sign of peace. I would suggest an annual national gathering on a large open space, and perhaps more frequent local gatherings since it is only by overcoming prejudices at the local level that real reunion can become possible.

"As a prisoner for the Lord, then, I urge you to live a life worthy of the calling you have received. Be completely humble and gentle; be patient, bearing with one another in love. Make every effort to keep the unity of the Spirit through the bond of peace. There is one body and one Spirit - just as you were called to one hope when you were called - one Lord, one faith, one baptism; one God and Father of us all, who is over all and through all and in all." St Paul (Ephesians 4:1-6).

Though I were standing alone, I would still proclaim this truth as the most important thing in the world. I would proclaim the power of love to do impossible things. No one believed a few years ago that the Berlin Wall could ever come down, and today how many Christians really believe and want the reunion in love which will melt the institutionalised walls of division? I have walked alone and exposed on the dividing walls of denomination (having experienced the Anglican, Roman Catholic, Baptist, Methodist and Orthodox communions in varying degrees). If I could, I would articulate the cry of my soul both for the pain and separation and grief of division and for the tremendous warmth and generosity of love which would fuse together the communion of saints.

Our Berlin Walls must come down. Brothers and sisters, together we must love them down.

Cambridge University Library
31 October 1996

Lincoln Cathedral Old Choristers 1995 Reunion

I like to think there may have been a saying amongst the Roman legions that all roads lead to Lincoln. It certainly appears that way as one looks at the map to plan the journey back, and it is easy to imagine that even then there was a sense of meeting and homecoming about this place. As you approach Lincoln from the south, the Roman roads seem to march over the hills in anticipation and excitement, and the Norman architects may have caught something of this spirit as they made the great arches which stride down the nave of the cathedral.

The garrison of old choristers who retraced their steps to Lincoln for the 67th reunion on 4th November last year came by a variety of routes, and were, no doubt, impelled by a variety of emotions. The reunion programme provided the traditional and excellent framework for the renewal of association with each other, with the cathedral and its music, and with Lincoln. All parts of the programme were of the usual excellent quality, and the day was for me, as I am sure for many others, one of the best spent days of the year.

Whenever I come to a reunion, I feel greatly privileged to have been a chorister at Lincoln and regret those times when I have not been able to come back. It is impossible to describe the range of feeling which the day calls forth, and it is perhaps best evoked in music rather than words. For me, the processional hymn at Evensong sung with lung-bursting passion, and the laying of the wreath sum it all up:

> From earth's wide bounds, from ocean's farthest coast,
> Through gates of pearl streams in the countless host,
> Singing to Father, Son and Holy Ghost,
> Alleluia! Alleluia!

We are not divided by the narrow stream of death, nor by any distance, whether physical or spiritual. So, on 4th November, as every year, the reunion extends its spirit to those who have passed on, and also to all absent friends.

Walking Into Lincolnshire

On a weekend when the sun shone and expected rain did not arrive I walked into Lincolnshire. Along the Wash Coast from West Lynn to Fosdyke Bridge, I walked along elevated sea defence banks between the outflows of the Great Ouse, Nene and Welland. I measured my progress by two small islands in the Wash, which seemed far larger than they appeared on the map. At night, I camped out between the defence bank and the strip of salt marsh bordering the sea, and watched a ship slipping silently over the Wash against a backdrop of winking lights and the starscape overhead.

I crossed the border from Norfolk into Lincolnshire on Saturday afternoon. At first, no difference. But then, as I reached the mouth of the Nene I noticed, etched against the surrounding fenland, an impressive line of autumnal trees on both banks. The afternoon seemed thick with silence lying over the land. Sutton Bridge seemed somehow different from Norfolk, and as I walked my way back to the coast along narrow winding lanes I noticed the familiar red brick of Lincolnshire houses. On one farm outbuilding was the emblem of Lincoln Cathedral, suggesting the influence of the county town even here in the furthest reaches of the fens.

Looking at the names on the map seemed to generate an impression of a land different in kind and quality from its neighbours. Looking coastwards: Holbeach Marsh, Frampton, Fishtoft, Butterwick Low, Boston Deeps. And then inland towards the fens and beyond: Wigtoft, Surfleet Seas End, Pinchbeck, Car Dyke, Sempringham. What is it about these names that seems to bring back, like an echo, a sense of light and peace as if washed and distilled out of a Lincolnshire sky? As I walked along those raised banks next to the sea, it was as if I was exposed in that strangely beautiful poetic region where sea and sky and Lincolnshire meet. This is a hallowed landscape, always seeming to point beyond itself to that which cannot be defined in water, air or land, and in which all elemental reality serves only as a symbol to recall the landscape of the soul, the simplicity of love.

Do We Need Nature?

"I will lift up mine eyes unto the hills, from whence cometh my help" Psalm 121:1

A few weeks ago, on a hot weekend in July, I travelled up to the Pennines to a place called Kettlewell. I parked my car in a field, got a few things together into a rucksack, and started walking in the evening sunshine. I crossed the River Wharfe, which was flowing like brown ale, and started up the side of Wharfedale. Freed from the car, and eager to get on to the moor top, I walked quickly uphill, only pausing to get my breath every now and again. Crossing outcrops of limestone I gradually gained height until I reached Old Cote Moor Top, a ridge of land around 2000 feet high running between Wharfedale and Littondale in the Yorkshire Dales National Park, England. [As a Yorkshireman once said to me on a previous visit to Wharfedale, "You've come to the reet part", and he was right].

At the top of the ridge, there is a dry stone wall which runs along the top, and leaving the main path, I began to follow the sheep tracks which run along the wall side. I was glad to be back on Old Cote Moor – this was a retracing of steps I had first taken a few years ago in equally brilliant sunshine. I continued to gain height, passing Birks Tarn, until I reached the triangulation point on Horse Head Moor. On my left was the massive bulk of Plover Hill and Pen-Y-Ghent on the other side of Littondale, with Ingleborough and Whernside further away. On my right was Buckden Pike over the other side of Wharfedale, and away beyond Buckden Pike were the Pennine hills rolling into the distance in the heat haze. A curlew called in the loneliness of the evening. There was no one else up here.

I carried on. I watched the red sun sink over Langstrothdale Chase, and walked on along the ridge in the afterglow, feeling that slight fear you feel when the sun has gone and you know night is coming and you are alone on the hills. In due course the dusk came, but it did not really get dark until around 11.30, and soon after this the moon came up. It was full, and by its light I continued to walk easily along the soft grass on the ridge top. It is easy walking in limestone country – the grass is soft and springy.

Around 12.30 pm, after an unexpected shock from an electric fence and about five hours walking, I reached my destination, the triangulation point on High Green Field Knott. I got out my sleeping bag, got inside and lay down facing across the dale towards Plover Hill. To my right was Cam Fell where the Roman Road ran over the top under the moonlight. Behind me were the hills of Langstrothdale; and above were the stars. The moon arched over Pen-Y-Ghent during the night, and set somewhere over Cam Fell. During the brief night, a few gusts of wind gently sighed over me from out of the dale, brushing over the top of High Green Field.

I was free out here; free from the proliferation of laws and restrictions, from urban chaos, from man-made tyrannies of one sort or another. Here I had the sound of the wind in the grass, the wild and wide open spaces in the hills, and only the sheep for company, and the cries of curlew and grouse hanging on the breeze.

In a democracy, perhaps it is the freedom of nature which is the most important freedom of all. There are now so many ways in which we are not free in our urban lives – is it any wonder that the "right to roam" has now come into force? It is needed. Up on the moors the sheep stare at you blankly as if failing to comprehend man who proliferates laws to the point where so many of them are completely unenforceable. Come into the wild and keep nature's law for a time.

There are only a few days of the year when it is warm enough to go up into the Pennines without a tent and sleep rough on the hills: I had taken my opportunity. I mentioned fear of
being alone. This passes with the realisation that you are most certainly not alone. Out here under the immense grandeur and beauty of the hills and star-scattered sky, you weep - I have done it – for the incredible beauty of which you are a part. You feel humbled, small – and something speaks to your soul. The free wind brushes your face, and washes your soul clean. I have kept faith with these hills, I have cried on their shoulders as if they were my friends, and I have laughed and skipped on them for sheer joy.

So, for the sake of freedom, and for the sake of knowing that we are not alone – don't you think it is strange that you can be alone on a hill and not feel lonely, yet in the middle of a city of millions and feel terribly lonely? - I think we do need nature. But does nature need us?

The odd thing about going off into the wild, especially going straight from a city, is the lack of people. What I mean is that there are so few people in the countryside, the landscape is empty. Since the Industrial Revolution, we are not only a highly urbanised society, but also now a polarised one. Most people do not now live in the countryside, close to nature – this is the exact opposite of the situation a couple of hundred years ago. This is a fact of such profound significance that is worthy of reflection. People live in cities yet go to designated National Parks or Areas of Outstanding Natural Beauty for their recreation – a polarised situation. People in the countryside, both inside and outside National Parks, feel neglected and misunderstood – witness the demonstrations of the Countryside Alliance in recent years.

Perhaps, therefore, we do need to repopulate rural areas to some degree, and thereby re-establish touch with the values, rhythms and cycles of nature. On the international scale we can see why this is important through issues such as global warming and deforestation. But on the national scale, does it make sense both economically and socially to have our population so unevenly distributed across the land, with the resultant pressures on urban centres and national parks? Whilst development is obviously going to be restricted to some degree inside national parks, should we not encourage rural repopulation more than we do, both inside and outside the parks? Perhaps it is fanciful, but I sometimes feel the land is calling us back, because it needs us. A landscape is lonely without people in it, not too many, but not too few either.

It began to get light around 2.30 am, a gentle lightening in the sky over Buckden Pike. I got up, put my sleeping bag away and began to walk back the way I had come. There was a light dew on the grass. I walked a little more slowly now, it was the light before dawn. The sun came up over the hills at what seemed the ridiculously early time of 4.50 am. It was John Hillaby who said that ecstasy is an unfashionable commodity. Yet this is out here, free, for anyone who will take the trouble. Perhaps this is why one does not feel lonely, you are out of yourself and inside nature, absolutely high on the intoxicating wind blowing gently through the grass on the free hills of England. It is a Welsh word, hiraeth, which means a longing for something distant or out of reach – this is what you feel out here, in touch with the longings of your soul, in touch with magnificent panoramas and the romance of hills rolling into the hazy distance of longing. We need this, we absolutely need it.

At moments like this, you understand completely why some people will fight so hard to stop encroachments into national parks, whether in the UK or anywhere else in the world. In the Pennines, there is the reservoir of Cow Green, which reduced the magnificent natural waterfall of Cauldron Snout to a regulated flow. There is a quarry in Upper Ribblesdale which is such an eyesore you can't help wondering how it was ever allowed.

Going back along the ridge in the brilliant Sunday morning sunshine I cannot exactly put it into words, but I felt privileged to have been out that night in the open. I think we do all need something of this kind of experience of nature. On the way back, I passed a sheep stuck in a bog – I hesitated before deciding to try to pull it out, and later felt guilty because I had hesitated, another urban trait, it is always somebody else's problem. But there was I face to face with a stuck sheep and nobody else for miles. I tested the bog, wound my tracksuit round the sheep's neck, cleared some peat away from around it, and pulled. It took a bit of work, but I got it out, and later felt really pleased with myself. If nothing else that day I had rescued a sheep.

That sheep seemed a metaphor for man stuck in his own mess, a metaphor for all man-made systems which ignore too much the forces of nature, but also for nature's need of man. We do need nature, and sometimes, perhaps paradoxically, nature needs us too.

Cricket – Inspiration, Art and Life

Cricket is inspiration. Just think of some of the great cricketing moments: Ian Botham's innings of 148 not out, in 1981 – surely one of the most stirring and inspiring sporting achievements of the last century. Apparently in a lost cause, that innings changed the course of the match and the series, and enabled England to regain the Ashes. It was the way Botham went about it. He fought back with spirit, determination, power and pugnacity – taking the fight to the Australians.

Cricket is art. Think of the spin bowling of Shane Warne – that famous ball which bowled Mike Gatting. Deception in flight, zip, fizz, wrenching finger and wrist spin. The run-up of Bishen Bedi – was it a run-up at all ? Just a few ambling steps. And what about the approach and delivery of Dennis Lillee – grace, power and poetry in motion; or the wisdom and skill in the bowling of Richard Hadlee. The late cut of a Vishwanath - the wrist movement worthy of an artist making strokes on a canvas. Viv Richards – erect poise, stepping forward into that easy stroke, ball timed in seconds to the boundary. Tendulkar.

Cricket is life. A strange combination of passion and patience. Atherton and Boycott – English grit, stubbornness and defence. Unfair dismissals – the lbw that wasn't. Second chances – but also cruel ends to careers. Different pitch and weather conditions. Play like the West Indians – hit the ball on the up – meet life head on and don't shy away. Or perhaps even better, play patiently to suit the mood of the day, the people, the weather – use your skill and experience, but never lose the passion which bursts out with the sheer exuberance and joy of the game, the fruit more of class and talent than of technical accomplishment. Think of Viv Richards suddenly bursting into a flurry of stroke play after a long and patient accumulation of runs, or Brian Lara's sheer pace of scoring.

A Walk from Land's End to John O' Groats - July to October 1991

Last summer, between 15 July and 18 October, the Department of the Environment granted me special leave to do a long distance walk from Land's End to John O' Groats to raise funds for a Christian prayer group, with which I am involved in London. I took the walk on as something of a personal, physical and spiritual challenge, as well as to help the prayer group. It took about three months to plan and organise, and I found, that my administrative training in the Civil Service came in useful in this respect. I had to plan a route, purchase equipment, arrange dates and times for eighteen friends and relations to join me on the walk; arrange to meet members of related prayer groups in Plymouth, Bristol, Birmingham, Manchester and Glasgow, and book accommodation in advance as far as Bristol. Training for the walk consisted of walking in to work in Marsham Street from north London, and, for inspiration, I read John Hillaby's "Journey through Britain", which I thoroughly recommend to anyone interested in walking.

I did the walk from south to north, using a combination of long distance footpaths, like the West Highland Way, and my own improvised routes, following for example, rivers such as the Wye, Severn and Tweed. The total mileage turned out to be about 1,100 completed in 83 walking days, with 13 rest days. After a wet spring in London, I was blessed with exceptionally fine weather, suffering only 36 hours of rain in the whole walk. I stayed mainly in youth hostels, 'Bed and Breakfasts' and with friends; my tent was dispensed with after two weeks as it proved too uncomfortable.

The main spiritual benefit of the walk was the sense of peace, space and silence. I enjoyed particularly the early part of the Pennine Way, where prolonged sunny weather had dried out even the sponge–like plateau of Kinder Scout, and one of the highlights of the walk was a view of the Pennines rolling away to the south from a hill called Shacklesborough on Stainmore. Another highlight, in Scotland, was a star-filled autumn sky above the Great Glen in which I saw, during the course of the night, the constellation of the Plough rotating and a number of stars shooting to the accompaniment of the stags, which had begun to roar by early October. The worst point of the walk, by contrast, was probably having to spend the night in an isolated croft outhouse in Inverness-shire and then getting lost in the mist the next morning. By good fortune and good care of my feet, I suffered no blisters during the entire walk – the main physical hazard seemed to arise in trying to negotiate stiles and gates without falling off. The mental challenge was, overall, greater than the physical, particularly during times alone, when it was harder to manage the distractions of what J B Priestley has called "the skull cinema".

Environmentally, I preferred the wilder, less 'planned' north, especially Stainmore and the northern Pennines, the West Highlands and the desolation of Sutherland. Litter was noticeably worse in Scotland, where a string of Irn-Bru cans seemed to border every minor road in the Lowlands.

Having started in sunshine, the walk finished, fittingly, in hail showers and high winds, interspersed with rainbows. Approximately £2,500 was raised for the prayer group, and I am grateful to the Department for allowing me the time to do the walk.

Land's End to John O'Groats 1991

(Poems written during walk)

Innocence - 14 July

Lost child
Lost innocence
Lost, lost
And all the time losing
Yet all this is my losing

And I forget my losing
And strain on
Towards the winning-post
Won for me
And there I shall find
Innocence again.

A Girl Playing in the Sand at Porthlawan Beach - 18 July

A little girl on the beach
Carried spadefuls of sand
From here to there
One after the other.

With each splashed spade
Came a pleased smile
As the graceful wind
Smoothed her young head.

How wonderful to be a child !
And to just know
What simple things to do
To bring pleasure
(To yourself and God)

O that we knew how to be
Children again
How to cry easily
And to be forgiven.

To let our emotions pass
Like cloud-shadows drifting.
And to feel enthusiasm
Burning in us.

And how wonderful to be helpless
And humble
In the face of all this
That we call Life.

Old Red Hotel - 19 July

Coming into Newquay
I saw an old red hotel
Against the grey sky,
Softly grey and salt sprayed,
The scene crashed by the sea.

The old building stood finely
Against the sky
Like a bastion, or an outpost
In some mysterious way.
And I felt welcomed
Into a common scene
A place where people come and go
And the years pass by
And the old building still stands.

A Field Above Porth Joke - 19 July

Soft field, Soft field,
Soft, Soft,
Soft as down
Soft as down
Soft with ripples of the wind

I wish I could lay my head down
In your softness
And cuddle down into you
Amongst the poppies

And the yellow flowers
And the downy grass
Into the folds of the land

Smoothed by summer breezes
Into a timeless world
Forever smoothed by
The soft peace of breezes.

Still Evening - 21 July

On a still evening
Everything is still
The trees are silent
And fields are green
Cows in them in the distance
Don't move much
And sheep rest
I can hear a few birds singing
And nearby horses chomping
But elsewhere
Peace settles calmly
Holding everything.

The road just trodden
Stretches back
Under the cool trees
There's peace on that road
Under the cool trees
A shady green peace
Sheltered there
Waiting, waiting.

Tired - 22 July

Sometimes I feel tired of life
An old man in a young body
So much pain, so much weariness
Weariness, Weariness
Tired, Tired.

I've run so far
Tried so hard
Yet it still seems so hard
Just to live.
Somehow, it's still just as hard
To cry out or make a fuss.
I still find myself
Smiling or bearing the pain silently
Despite, behind my eyes,
A growing anguish.

Full Moon - 26 July
(Sitting near bridge at Bellover)

The sky is vast with God.
The full moon is bright white
Against the hill.
And the water smoothes slowly
Catching the evening-still light.

Only the small churning of the water
Against the silence of the sky.
Elsewhere peace,

I feel so tired within –
Exhausted from so much violent running.
How right it is to be still,
Quiet, how right for the soul.

Surely it is right with God
For me to be still,
To stop running,
To gradually wind down.

Slow down, let the
Peace of the countryside seep
Into you …
God made all this beauty,
But, like us, he made it for
Himself.
We must worship God.

Trusting - 26 July

This evening I saw a blind girl
Being led.
She was so beautiful in her
Helplessness
I thought this is how we are
With God,
How we must come,
Smiling but lost,
Holding our hand out trusting
Braving the hurts
But trusting, trusting
Like children.

1 John - 26 July

O Love
Thank you for coming to my soul
Tonight.
O Love, I have lost you
Since I am condemned to wander
In this dark place

Yet your memory echoes within me
And I hunger for you
In my innermost parts
O Love please come
And cleanse all the defilement's
Of this dark house of flesh

Having come, so silently O Love
I hardly know you are here
Yet now I am humbled
By your soft presence

And I hold you silently, peacefully
For you, O Love
Are God.

I Came - 26 July

It was sinners I came to save
Not righteous men
I came for those
So defiled in their own eyes
They do not even think to
Speak my name
Yet I would go to them
If they spoke it

I came for men locked in fetters
Made for me to shatter –
My power is explosive yet gentle
A consuming fire, yet peace.

I came for you
To draw you to me
Will you come now ?

Blind Girl - 27 July

Today I said Hello
To a blind girl
I didn't know whether to.
It was hard to take that first step
Towards someone
Taking a risk.
Having taken it,
The look of joy in her face
And the way she lit up
As she acknowledged my greeting
Was so beautiful
That, later,
I *wanted* to cry.
I am so grateful to her
Because
She helped me accept myself.
The way she sat apart
Was like my inner self
The child inside me

Who is so frightened
Of being rejected.
Yet she wasn't frightened
When I spoke to her
Like a flower opening up
To the sun
She responded.

Creacombe Moor - 29 July

Wind in the trees.

Wind in the trees.

Space on the hills.

The trees rustle in their space
On the hills

And they stay there tomorrow.

A Lovely Mother - 1 August

Today I met
A lovely mother
Gentle and quietly spoken
Perhaps underneath she was shy
But didn't show it.
She left me with a feeling of Love
Which warmed me through.
I hardly spoke to her
Yet I'll remember her
And she wished me luck
With my walking
God bless, God bless this lady.

How lonely people are.
I could tell the way she spoke
There was so much more behind the words
That meeting though so brief
Was *very* deep.

Outside Crowcombe Youth Hostel

In distant trees birds sing their evening song
A lone dog barks intermittently
And rabbits sit quietly in the fields
Across the lawn sits silence

It waits under the trees for dark to come
And gradually the shadows grow.
In this space of grass,
Surrounded by trees
In the still evening
I find peace.
Breaths of wind come and
Waver through the trees.
Gently, gently comes the dark.

Two Children

I felt a healing love tonight.
I was bubbling with laughter inside.
Two children danced and played
And how wonderful their playing was
To me.

Steve smiled, threw himself on the floor,
Laughed, a bundle of energy.
How happy to be alive.
Sarah, older, more confident,
Was easily free with her actions.
This love that I felt came to me
From the children, and parents too
There was a love between all of them
Holding them all, covering the space between them
And for me this love
Covered the sight of my sins from my inward gaze
How strange that deep pains should
So easily
Be washed by waves of Love
This, this is the only thing which heals
The only patience, the only kindness

Love.
Wash me, fill me again and again
Sweet Love
Flow into my darkness and consume it.

Love

Lord, today I felt humbled.
I admitted to someone
That I don't understand
Much of the Bible and what
People call 'Doctrine'
And that I didn't like the
Bits about 'Hell'.

What I can understand is
Love
And Love which died for me.
Lord please understand I am only a child
I have not yet grown up.
I discuss so many things with people
And present a proud front so often
But really I am a little child inside
And Lord I thank you for speaking to me
In words I can understand.
A child understands Love
Its touch, its face, its presence,
It seems so strange
That so many people spend so long
Talking about you
As if they didn't know you
And because they can't find you
In their lives.
Yet you are there, they just can't see you.

Lonely

How lonely I feel
Waves of loneliness come
Accompanied by sadness
My inside feels almost drenched with it
Somehow it purges
Somehow it fills the stomach
But I need something to fill this aching void, quench it.
Only Love can quench it.

Wind of Grace - 9 August

The wind of grace blows
Like breeze across the water
Like white swans gliding
So easily, so easily.
So often we get lost in our own currents
So that we cannot come to the surface of our lives
And receive.

I Felt So Sad - 10 August

I felt so sad
This afternoon
It would have been easy
To have turned aside
To familiar ways
Of escaping,
Somehow though
The emotion held me.
I felt washed in sadness
And somehow staying with it
Cleansed me.

My Own Girl - 10 August

Today I saw
A girl
Sitting on a park bench.
When will I be the one
To go and greet
My own girl
Sitting on a park bench
Waiting for me.
Will I ever be the one ?
Lord, it seems so long.
Is there a girl somewhere
Who will love me ?
Lord, I know you love me
But I need a special someone.
My own girl.

Walk in His Time

Love yourself,
Love yourself, do
It may be harder than you think
To treat yourself with respect
To care about the little things
To force yourself to make time, slow down
Stop, rushing
So you can catch up with yourself
You may want to keep on going frantically.
But you're only running away with yourself
You can't go that fast
You'll burn yourself out.
Take time each day
To walk, walk slowly.

With God.
His hand is sure, His touch gentle,
Put your hand in His
And walk in His time
He is there, all the time
Ever so quietly.

Malvern Hills - 12 August

Today I saw
Some high silent clouds
Gazing across a landscape.
Light streamed through them
From patches of brilliant blue.

Looking down from the hill
I heard the sound of cars.
Once no cars could be heard
From this hill
And the landscape was different
But many people have stood
And from here seen the streaming light.

Silence On The Hills

Silence on the hills
And sun shining on corners
Of green fields.
Clouds high above the plain
Woods hugging folds of land
Huddled houses
Breeze blowing gently
Up the hill
Through the fading grass
Of late summer.
And me here and the road
Stretching out before me.

Its so quiet here
How quiet it is
How quietly the land lies sat
Before me.

Shafts of light fall from the clouds.

Three Girls - 13 August

I said 'Hello'
To three young girls
Yesterday.

I told them
I was on holiday,
Walking.
They had come from Birmingham.

How wonderful is the chance meeting
When we speak light words,
When we come to the surface of ourselves.
How wonderful it was
Just to exchange a few words.

I was sorry when,
Next morning,
They left before I could say
Goodbye.

Let Me Sing

It is early morning,
Still,
The river is calm
And the woods on the other bank
Are bathed in sunshine.
Birds are singing in the still morning
And the stillness hangs
Only slowly passing.

Waves of different memories
Come to me.
The cheerful song of a small bird
High above in the blue sky
Recalls my soul's innocence
I used to sing like that in my heart
More often.

Lord help me to sing like that again
Today
And not to get lost
In tracks that lead nowhere.

Bring joy to my heart, Lord
And gratitude for all your benefits

O Lord, put a new song into my heart
Let me sing, let me sing
For I was made to sing
And soar like a bird.

Pain

Sometimes I feel cynical
Nothing can really change my life
Make the pain pass
Make it possible to live.

I know I have to let
My cynicism go.
To be happy I can't be sad
It seems so simple
And yet
It is hard to sing
And wear a smile
When the heart within
Is so much in pain
So wounded.

It seems so false
To be happy when you're not.
But then I think
Do I need a reason to be happy ?
Why should I not sing
Even though my heart hurts ?
I am alive
And life, painful life, is wonderful.

O God, dissolve my pride

And let me sing
And listen to my broken song.
And if I cry,
Let my tears wash the pain away.

Arriving at Kidderminster - 15 August

There's a breeze blowing today
A warm and gentle breeze
Through the trees.
It seems to carry my cares
Away
Like dandelion down

And the leaves wave on the branches
As if beckoning
Fresh life from me.

There is a lightness in the breeze.
My poor spirit can only faintly feel it.
But it is there for the heart
Ready to be
Light enough.

It's Nearly Autumn - 20 August

Mist on early morning fields
Takes me back
To a half remembered boyhood,
It hangs low
Near the woods
It's nearly autumn.

A Buzzing Bee

A buzzing bee
Flew by me today,
Landed on my book
And went lazily
Head over heels,

A fumbling bumbling bee
With no cares
Except
Making honey.

Thank You

Thank you (Lord) for the birds
Thank you for the grass
Thank you for the trees
Thank you for the bees
Buzzing past.

Thank you for love
Thank you for play
Thank you for praise
Thank you for your Face
Smiling today.

On The Pennines - 31 August

It's silent here
Except for the distant cry
Of sheep in the valley.
The blue sky is vast
Far the gentle drone of an aeroplane
And the buzzing of bees
Near me
And the gentleness of the breeze
Carries summer here
To me.

Summer is here now
In this unlikely place
Usually windswept and lonely
Now open to the sky
Revealed
And bathed in sunshine
Here in the hills
The summer hills

There is peace.
Everything is mellowed
And I am gently laid down
On the grass
There is time here
Time to rest.

Out Here - September

Out here,
On the hills
I feel the grace of God

The birds are singing for joy
As the sun climbs slowly up the sky
And the green hills drop into the valleys,
Squares of green divided by perennial walls
Hilltops clothed in purple heather
And a breeze blowing gently -
The cries of sheep.

All this is just here.
I am here, by chance, this morning
I didn't seek this beauty,
It came to me.

Somehow, God is here
I cry for the pain of this beauty
Coming to me
Beckoning forth
The heaped up layers of sadness
And I can but give them to Him

And then my spirit soars
Higher than the hills
With the brilliance of flashing fire.

Silence - September

Broken words
Are all that will come.

Struggling for expression
The voice fails

Silence seems to absorb my words
And there seems nothing to say.

The fight to speak seems violent
And I do not want people to hear
Instead of words,
Violence.

So I say little
And allow the vast hinterland
Of (struggling) unspoken words
To remain unsaid.

Yet, somehow, the few words spoken
Speak the depth of
Silence behind.

A Rainbow Dances - September

A rainbow dances in the sky
Spanning across my cares,
And I look again
And my cares seem less
Against the bright colours.

A rainbow dances in the sky
Arching across my pains,
And I look again
And my pain is transformed
By the beauty stretching across.

A rainbow dances in the sky
Dancing around my tears

And I look again
Through a spectrum of tears
And a new covenant is made with joy.

How To Speak To You - September

I wanted to spend
Half an hour
With you this morning
I could only manage 5 minutes.

I didn't know how to speak to you
Or what to say
Or whether words were necessary

I was worried, indecisive
I was so worried how I'd do it
I didn't do it at all.

Later on I felt small
In the summer afternoon
There was peace, a gentle breeze,
And the freedom of beautiful surroundings,
I felt you say
I have given you all this
Why worry about how to speak.

Just be with me
And do what you can
Don't speak at all
Keep silence
Feel only the warmth of my presence
And leave the trying to me.
You try too hard
I feel pain when I see
Your face tightened with effort
I'm bigger and stronger than you
And remember you are with me
Not on your own.

We must pray together.

Strathmore Arms (Lunch Time) - 9 September

I sat in a garden,
Almost alone.
Only a man drinking beer
Was there.
This garden was quiet
Far off well-trodden roads.

Holding the scene
The English summer,
Gently warming
And giving back peace, freedom
All is held, just held.

The gently blowing breeze says
Wait, wait awhile with me
Be slow with me.
Slow.

Upper Teesdale - September

This river is beautiful
The sun lights up its surface
And rocks create white bubbles
On the brown water,
Like beer.

Only I am here
To see this beauty now
I will pass, but the beauty will remain

Somehow, this morning
I don't feel alone
This beauty, meant to be shared,
Shares me.

The Love I Need

Love, gentle love
Comes silently to my heart
Amidst the fury and confusion
And the anger and the pain
And the violence of desire
It comes, the silent visitor,
The unseen guest

Can I make Him welcome
Or will the tyrannous flesh
Burst out again ?
Can I, like a little child,
Reach out to receive
The love I need ?

The question recedes
As the arms go out
On both sides.

Trees of Autumn. (Uswayford to Kirk Yetholm) - 16 September

Away from the end of the road
I see high clouds
With bright edges
Above low green hills
Holding the trees of autumn.

The wind blows hard
Through the foreground
But the trees of autumn
In the distance are still
Waiting for me to come (& see)
Before they shed their leaves.

Tomorrow I will go
To the trees of autumn
But, already, now, this scene carries away with it
The brown shrivelled leaves of my cares

Tomorrow, though, I will go
To the trees of autumn.

Staying With Pain - September

Today
My pain was very great.
But I stayed with my pain
Waiting for it to lessen
So that I could breathe
And see it more clearly.
Surely God would take it away
Eventually.

He did.
The pain lessened.
Sometimes the only way
Is to stick it out
The painful stabs,
The mental torture,
The agony
Believing
And hoping.
It's hard
Because it's always
Much easier
To find a quick solution
To take the pain away.

But staying with pain
Is good.
As you feel the dull ache pass
You feel life return
And you feel good again,
You feel
Joy.
And you stick through that pain,
And if you can pray
Just a little prayer
Then the dark cloud of pain
Gains

A silver lining
Not much
Only 'Please God'
Or 'Help me'.

He hears
Yes, He hears.

And your pain becomes beautiful.
And your smile of joy
When your pain passes
Is lovely.

Sometimes I feel cleansed
By the agony of pain
It has wrung me dry.
But my tears
Have washed me.

Bydlo - September

The cart moves
Slowly across the hill
Wheels turning, creaking.

Horizon changes
The dark sky looms, so dark
So dark
The line of the hill slowly changes

The cart advances
Where is the movement taking it
Where is the cart going ?
I don't know, no one knows,
Just a cart moving

Somehow the moving cart
Against the hill
Under the dark sky
Fills with awe.

Suddenly the Cross appears
Against the dark sky
Three figures bleeding
Against the dark sky

The cart passes
And recedes into the distance.
The dark sky
And the bleeding figures
And the Cross
Are left ...

The Sun is Shining

Today the air is cold
But the sun is shining
Between the high white clouds
The birds are singing
In the still landscape
Cows stand peacefully in the green,
A man walks by
And tells me he's going for a bus
'It's a lovely day' he says
And how lovely the day is.
Autumn shadows lengthen
Beneath the trees
As the day ages, passes,
Slowly passes
And the great high clouds
Sit on the sky majestically
And the fields roll away
To a hazy distance.

Today - September

Hope speaks
From a blue sky
And white clouds
And fresh rain-washed woods.

Today is a new day
Why live in yesterday ?
All that is past is gone
Never to return.
The heart loves to live
Today.

Caledonian Canal above Loch Oich - October

The breeze caresses the trees gently.
Below, the canal water
Spreads wind-skimmed ripples
Across its black surface.
Above, the sun sheds
Glistening rays on to the water.

The breeze lovingly rocks the trees
And they sway so gently
As some of their leaves fall
In to the water.

I feel privileged to be here
As the wind quietly rustles the trees.
How lightly they dance.

On The Way to Bhlaraidh

I feel so strangely comforted
By the sound of running water
In the stream beside which I sit.
It just keeps running on
Bubbling and eddying and falling
It seems to mingle with my troubled thoughts
And calm them.
Somehow all I feel is sadness.
I know I have failed God again,
And I do feel remorse and repentance now.
And I feel this forgiving touch
Again on me.
It is beautiful here besides the stream

There are some old mossed trees
Which are very still
And yellow-brown October bracken
Still wet and glistening
In the afternoon sun.
Somehow I don't feel alone here
I don't feel alone.
Strange that.
Because I am alone – there's no one else here.
I feel very old and tired and hurt
But not alone

Cradling myself here
Yes, perhaps feeling a little sorry for myself,
I can just about accept my life.

Midnight - October

Here
The stars seem to stretch back
Over the sky
Over the way I've come
So many miles back.
The milky way splashes
Across the sky

I've come all that way
And now I'm here
And tonight I see
The clear sky splashed with stars
Stretching back, stretching back
Over the way I've come
Like a million jewels
Spangling the sky

Their silent beauty
Stretches back, stretches back
Over the way I've come.

It's a beautiful sky
Stretching back

Over the time, I've been,
Over the miles,
Over the pain
But now a beautiful starlit sky
Stretching back and back ..

Only Me - October

In the stillness of an October morning
I see the reds and yellows and browns
Of the trees and bracken,
The clouds hang low on the hills
And when I breathe
My breath makes a mist in the air.
The stags are roaring on the hills
And just now I saw a herd running.
I feel the space of the early morning
And there is no one else here.
Only me and all this beauty.

Below Loch Locky - October

Wind lashed autumn trees
Blow and surge
Their leaves away
The wet leaves fly
On the rushing wind
As the rushing wind blows big
Through the trees
A crescendo of rushing
Invisible wind
Branches dancing and waving
Leaves flying off,
Showered with rain,
The sound of autumn blowing.

Wet yellow and brown leaves
Lie on the ground
On the bank under the trees
On the green moss.

The year is falling
As the leaves fall from the trees
Again this year
Fluttering and falling
As the clouds hang low in the sky
And the wind lashes the trees
With fury
How they withstand the rushing, lashing wind
Whoosh! Whoosh! It blows
Blowing itself into a crescendo
Of wet leaf-filled noise.

Crescendo, crescendo
Rush, lash, furious wind blowing
Bashing, lashing, crashing the trees
In (truth) a crescendo of anger.
The flying wind blows and blows
Through the trees.

Sutherland

Sitting on a road in Sutherland
Having walked many many miles
I feel on top of the world.
It is autumn and the sun is shining
On the lochs
The breeze is blowing across the moors
And white clouds sit in distant hills
A breath of summer blows back
The memories of former days
Here, here is peace
A long slow, patient peace
Softly
Layered over time,
It is here, it is here
Patient peace.

ROBBIE'S ROUTE   1,100 miles

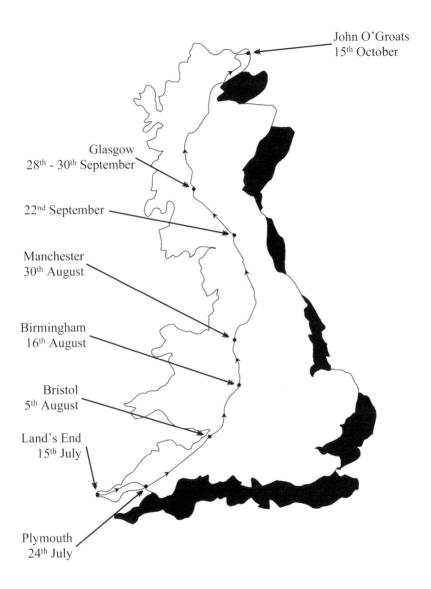

John O'Groats
15th October

Glasgow
28th - 30th September

22nd September

Manchester
30th August

Birmingham
16th August

Bristol
5th August

Land's End
15th July

Plymouth
24th July

Epilogue

The End of the Pilgrimage *

Lincoln Cathedral Cloister

My pilgrimage has ended now
To Lincoln I've returned
Gentle light on limestone; sheltered peace.

My pilgrimage has ended now
My soul to Lincoln has returned
And I'll renew my childhood vow
When my singing heart with passion burned
To love this place of peace and rest
Of light and grace so free.

*   Robbie's ashes were interred in the Lincoln Cathedral Cloister on
30 September 2004